DEDAH QUEEN

DEDAH QUEEN

A Memoir

Told by: Eliza Marcus

authorHOUSE®

AuthorHouse™
1663 Liberty Drive
Bloomington, IN 47403
www.authorhouse.com
Phone: 1-800-839-8640

*This is a work of fiction. All of the characters, names, incidents, organizations, and dialogue in
this novel are either the products of the author's imagination or are used fictitiously.*

First published by AuthorHouse 05/12/2011

ISBN: 978-1-4567-6412-8 (sc)

Library of Congress Control Number: 2011906926

Printed in the United States of America

*Any people depicted in stock imagery provided by Thinkstock are models,
and such images are being used for illustrative purposes only.
Certain stock imagery © Thinkstock.*

This book is printed on acid-free paper.

Dadah Queen

Revealing untold family secrets, for the very first time, will cause you to laugh, cry, and become a part of these special people. The results of these never before shared stories will become therapeutic for the family and inadvertently encourage you the curious reader.

The story of "Dedah Queen" (pronounced "dere the queen") begins with a girl who was a "Gullah" speaking African American, living in Cross, South Carolina, who became a hard working mother, and grandmother. Her wisdom will make you shake your head as you read how she worked as a housemaid living on $25.00 dollars a week, in the twentieth century. Her survival as a spiritual woman who played the piano at church by day, and the "boogie woogie," in her private chambers by night, will no doubt bring tears to your eyes. A deep dark secret of romance will unfold. And finally, with no formal education, this lovely lady left "common sense" sayings about life for all of us to use and to be encouraged by.

Are you the family historian? Then this is the book for you. Have you ever wanted to get to the root of your family's history? This book is a compilation of three generations made available with family trees, revealing untold family secrets...

Mariah "Dadah Queen" Brown Montgomery

Introduction

My name is Eliza Marshell Marcus, and I am the grand-daughter of Mariah "Dedah Queen", Montgomery. In order understand this book with greatest comprehension, you must first become like a pair of binoculars equipped with zoom optical lenses. By living with my grandmother, I was able to observe and be a part of three generations. I find this amazing because I'm only thirty nine years old, as of this writing, and yet I've seen more than the average person of my age. This triad involves my grandmother's way of living, my mother's way of living, and finally, my way of living, which have compelled me to believe that our patterns are one. I hope these stories will help you grow in wisdom. While writing this book, I saw people, languages, traditions, customs, dietary patterns, fashions, family involvement, religious intents, the economy, love, health issues, marriage, death, occupation, good and bad times. I wish to tell you, not too much has changed over the year, and most of all, I'm a witness to this fact. My single desire is that families who read this book get as much out of it as I did in writing it. So, if you are ready to be enlightened, and encouraged clean your binocular zoom lens then, please turn to the next page!

A map of surrounding cities in South Carolina

Cross, South Carolina in the early 1900s

Life as it was in Cross, South Carolina in the early 1900s was typical of the south. In 1918, Armistice Day brought about the end of World War I. The United States received no gain; the country only inherited heavy debt and the knowledge that all it sacrificed was in vain. Therefore, the Governor of South, Carolina, Olin D. Johnson, designated and proclaimed the week of November 4 to 11, 1938 as American Legion Week. This was, to set aside to invite citizens to join in the movement and educational program for "enduring peace," as stated by the Berkeley Democrat, in Moncks Corner, South Carolina November 3, 1938. While the state of South Carolina was enduring peace, Dedah Queen my grandmother had endured child-birth and had two children to think about. In 1937, Cross was faced with an epidemic of tuberculosis. Cross is located thirty five miles from Charleston, South Carolina. Although Cross was very small the community shared information in the local paper. The column was under the heading County News. Here are some of the announcements of that time: Mr. And Mrs. XYZ and family visited Mrs. ABC's mother, in Bonneau. Or, Mr. XYZ and son were visitors here Sunday. Professor ABC and his wife were visitors to the Charleston Fair. November 10, 1936. Your business was everybody's business. This column, County News, still exists.

Cross faced its share of racial tensions in 1938. Late Saturday afternoon, the home of Mr. And Mrs. XYZ of Cross was shot into. Immediate help arrived, and it was uncovered that random shooting were just some of the, troubles Negros had to endure. In 1939, Roosevelt Franklin was the President of the United States of America. He too asked the United States for no blackout of peace in this country, a thought shared by the governor of South Carolina, Olin D. Johnson, in 1938.

The rich soil of Cross was ideal for cotton, potatoes, corn and many other nourishing crops. Cross was where Dedah Queen grew up with her family. That was her home, and she always let others know that.

The public schools in Cross were for the rich. According to the Berkeley newspaper, the parents would take their children to one location to meet the school bus. However, their children would have a suitcase packed to stay in dorms for an entire week. At the end of the week, the parents would meet and pick up their children. Following is a survey of blacks and whites attending and finishing school beginning in 1920.

NUMBER OF HIGH SCHOOL GRADUATES, 1920-1940

Year	White Diplomas	Black Diplomas	Total Diplomas
1920	745	0	745
1925	3,716	0	3,716
1930	5,542	104	5,646
1935	7,974	303	8,277
1940	10,717	1,009	11,726

This chart was created by Daniel, "Public Education" 189-190

As a result of increased funding, more young Carolinians had the opportunity to obtain, genuine high school educations. Even though there were several excellent black high schools, such as Booker T. Washington in Columbia, no young black man or woman received a diploma until 1930 when three black high school students from Booker T. Washington, were recognized by the State Department of Education.

Jippy and Rhinah Brown

Jippy and Rhinah Brown were the parents of Mariah, "Dedah Queen", Brown. They found themselves nestled together in Cross, South Carolina during the nineteenth century. They were loved parents who had a total of five children. They were not well off. They lived in an old shanty house all of their lives. Their conveniences were limited but their love was eternal. Yes, sometimes they used newspapers to cover the inside walls of the house. I dare suggest Jippy and Rhinah did without; I'll simply say that they made adjustments when necessary to their circumstances. Isn't that what we do today? They were farmers, herbalist, and a barber amongst many other occupations required for survival. Working more than one job didn't merely start in these modern times but during the late 1900s, with Jippy and Rhinah Brown.

They ingrained hard work in the minds of all five children, along with manners. They say "manners will carry you further than any degree." Their children were all well behaved and they made sure their offsprings did likewise. Many courtesies were often extended when guests came over, like offer your guest something to eat or drink or entertain your company with music or such that you have. Make your company feel welcome and comfortable. Jippy and Rhinah Brown lived a very simple life and yet, they made an impact on the lives of the next generation.

Dedah Queens' Siblings

Dedah Queen, had four siblings: Mary Brown, Freddie Brown, Sibbie Brown, and James Brown. Each sibling was gifted with his or her own special talents.

Mary Brown, the oldest of Jippy and Rhinah Brown's children, was an admirable example of an apothecary or modern-day herbalist or even a "root" doctor. Mary could create many different antidotes from plants, roots, and seeds that would cure various sicknesses. Her mother, Rhinah, handed down this tradition. People in the community knew of Mary's talent from family members and church members. A typical day for a great herbalist like Mary would start early in the morning just when the dew had moistened the earth. To prepare herself she wore an apron, the one that looped over the head and through the arms, pulling the body like a girdle to one's skin. The back of the apron had a bow, and in the front were two pockets, big enough to hold lots of plants, roots, and seeds. Mary extracted "head knot" from the swamps, a flower used for people who were slow learners. "Life everlasting" is a flower used to overcome flu symptoms. "Star root" is a plant used for pain such as cramps. These plants, roots, seeds, anise, and back bone roots all had multi-purpose uses.

Mary and "Dedah Queen," looked so much alike. This held true even at Mary's funeral when a young boy said, "Mary's not dead! She's sitting over there in that chair," pointing to "Dedah Queen." I remember several adults trying to explain to the boy that "Dedah Queen" was Mary's sister. The oddest thing about these sisters who looked so much alike was that they both died on Valentine's Day.

Freddie Brown, the second oldest was called the dreamer. He was Moses Brown's father. Freddie had the ability to interpret dreams and many people including his family relied on his interpretations. I remember "Dedah Queen" saying that if an alcoholic was in your dream the only way to get rid of him was to pour some whiskey on the ground; he would drink it and leave your dream. I'm sure her brother Freddie would have shared these type stories with the family from time to time.

Sibbie Brown, the third child, who was short and medium-built, was the seamstress. Her parents were able to buy her an old sewing machine. She made clothes and other items without using a pattern. Let's say you wanted a man's suit. Sibbie would look at your body structure while taking a few measurements. Next, you would verbally describe in detail to her how you wanted your suit to look. Within a week Sibbie would have you in a suit tailored for a king. Sibbie still sews today even in her nineties.

James Brown, the fourth child was the musician. Like Sibbie his parents were able to buy what was needed to practice his talent. In his case it was an organ. It was Jippy's idea to get the organ, although not instrumental himself. The old organ was made by, a company called "Chiery." It was about four feet tall and three feet wide, small enough to fit in most rooms. The redwood texture organ had a crafty freeze on its panel below the keys. The organ had eleven diapasons and one row of keys totaling roughly seventy-three black and white keys. Still not enough to be considered a standard keyboard, Two large foot pedals were, in the center near the floor allowing the volume to increase or decrease. The seat was a stool with the top capable of turning three-hundred-sixty degrees. It resembled the stools depicted at a piano, in the Western saloons or vaudeville shows. Dedah Queen took her first organ lesson from her brother James. She too became a wonderful musician.

Moses, Freddie's son, and Dedah Queen's nephew, talked about religious music at their church Zion United Methodist Church during the mid 1900's as a way to remind people of their sins. For example, Moses said, "If a person was cheating on his/her spouse the church members would repeatedly sing this song, "Time Will Bring You In." If anyone smoked they would sing the, "Tobacco Song."

Chewing Tobacco
Smoking Cigarettes
You Better Quit Cause
When You Get To Heaven
They'll Be Nowhere To Spit.

Lyrics, like these were surely a great addition to songs. Moses said the music would get so intense, that people would begin dancing and shouting. Not only did the worship service have order but church procedure did, too. Moses said the members of Zion would sponsor a "Penny Rally," where everyone would turn in as many pennies possible. When the pennies were collected, the church treasurer would ask the pastor for his handkerchief (the pastor was never allowed in the same room with the money). The treasurer would then scoop up two or three big handfuls of pennies tie them in the handkerchief and give them to the pastor (this was the pastor's salary). Moses said this money would last the pastor for several weeks, because things didn't cost very much.

Key to Symbols

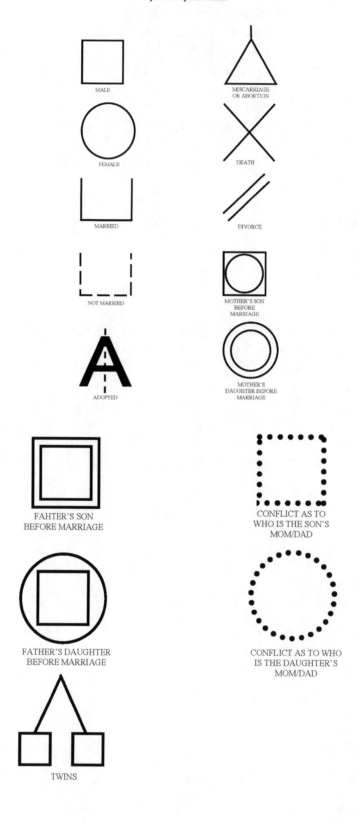

MALE

FEMALE

MARRIED

NOT MARRIED

ADOPTED

FAHTER'S SON
BEFORE MARRIAGE

FATHER'S DAUGHTER
BEFORE MARRIAGE

TWINS

MISCARRIAGE
OR ABORTION

DEATH

DIVORCE

MOTHER'S SON
BEFORE
MARRIAGE

MOTHER'S
DAUGHTER BEFORE
MARRIAGE

CONFLICT AS TO
WHO IS THE SON'S
MOM/DAD

CONFLICT AS TO WHO
IS THE DAUGHTER'S
MOM/DAD

Mariah Brown's Parents/Siblings

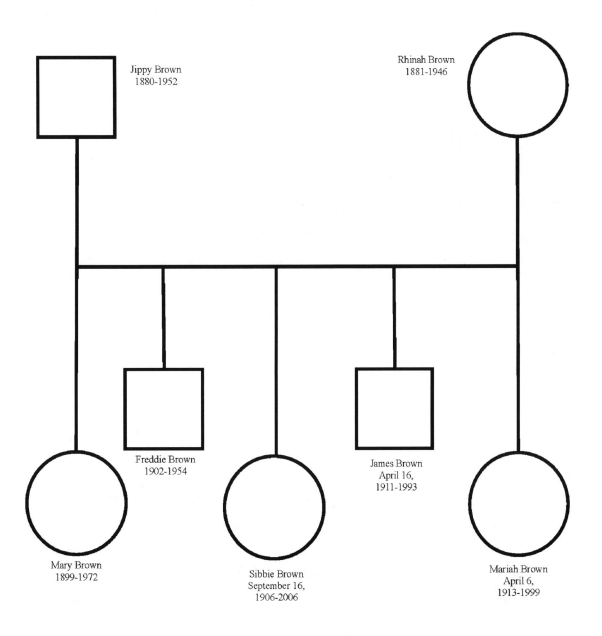

Jippy Brown
1880-1952

Rhinah Brown
1881-1946

Freddie Brown
1902-1954

James Brown
April 16,
1911-1993

Mary Brown
1899-1972

Sibbie Brown
September 16,
1906-2006

Mariah Brown
April 6,
1913-1999

UNITED STATES DEPARTMENT OF COMMERCE

July 16, 1976

UNITED STATES DEPARTMENT OF COMMERCE
Social and Economic Statistics Administration
BUREAU OF THE CENSUS
Washington, D.C. 20233

OFFICE OF THE DIRECTOR

Re:

Maria Montgomery

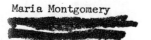

The following information, including spelling of name, relationship, age, etc., is an EXACT COPY of the census record as reported by the census taker on the original schedule.

Census of _____1920_____, taken as of _____January 1_____

County _____Berkeley_____ State _____South Carolina_____

Name	Relationship	Age	Place of birth	Citizenship
Brown, Maria	Daughter	7	South Carolina	

enumerated in the family of Jippy and Rhina Brown

☐ If checked, refer to footnote(s) _____ on reverse side of form.

Bureau of the Census

The above information is furnished in accordance with Title 13, United States Code, Section 8.

The Bureau of the Census does not issue birth certificates, but this record is often accepted in place of one.

FORM BC-655 (1-31-75)

12

CERTIFICATE OF DEATH

STATE OF SOUTH CAROLINA
DEPARTMENT OF HEALTH AND ENVIRONMENTAL CONTROL
CERTIFICATE OF DEATH

STATE BIRTH NUMBER					STATE FILE NUMBER

DECEDENT'S NAME First	Middle	Last	SEX	DATE OF DEATH (Month, Day, Year)
1. MARIA		MONTGOMERY	2. Female	3. February 14, 1999

SOCIAL SECURITY NUMBER	AGE - Last Birthday (Years)	UNDER 1 YEAR		UNDER 1 DAY		DATE OF BIRTH (Mo., Day, Year)	BIRTHPLACE (City, and State or Foreign Country)
	5a. 85	Months 5b.	Days	Hours 5c.	Minutes	6. April 6, 1913	7. CROSS, SC

WAS DECEDENT EVER IN U.S. ARMED FORCES? (Yes or No)	9a. PLACE OF DEATH (Check only once; see instructions on other side)
8. No	HOSPITAL: ☒ Inpatient ☐ ER/Outpatient ☐ DOA OTHER: ☐ Nursing Home ☐ Residence ☐ Other (Specify)

FACILITY NAME (If not institution, give street and number)	CITY, TOWN, OR LOCATION OF DEATH	COUNTY OF DEATH
9b. McLeod Regional Medical Center	9c. Florence	9d. Florence

MARITAL STATUS - Married, Never Married, Widowed, Divorced (Specify)	SURVIVING SPOUSE (If wife, give maiden name)	DECEDENT'S USUAL OCCUPATION (Give kind of work done during most of working life. Do not use retired.)	KIND OF BUSINESS/INDUSTRY
10. Widowed	11.	12a. Domestic	12b. Self Employed

RESIDENCE - STATE	COUNTY	CITY, TOWN, OR LOCATION	STREET AND NUMBER	INSIDE CITY LIMITS? (Yes or No)
13a. SC	13b. Florence	13c. FLORENCE	13d. 322 C ROYAL ST.	13e. Yes

ZIP CODE	Was Decedent of Hispanic Origin? (Specify Yes or No - If yes, specify Cuban, Mexican, Puerto Rican, etc.)	RACE - American Indian, Black, White, etc. (Specify)	DECEDENT'S EDUCATION (Specify only highest grade completed) Elementary/Secondary (0-12)	College (1-4 or 5+)
13f. 29506	14. ☐ Yes ☐ No (Specify)	15. Black	16. 6	

FATHER'S NAME First	Middle	Last	MOTHER'S NAME First	Middle	Maiden Surname
17. Jippy		Brown	18. Rinah		

INFORMANT'S NAME (Type/Print)	MAILING ADDRESS (Street and Number or Rural Route Number, City or Town, State, Zip Code)
19a. ███████	19b. ███████

METHOD OF DISPOSITION	PLACE OF DISPOSITION (Name of cemetery, crematory, or other place)	LOCATION - (City or Town, State)
20a. ☐ Burial ☐ Cremation ☐ Removal from State ☐ Donation ☒ Other (Specify)	20b. ZION UM CHURCH CEMETERY	20c. CROSS, S.C.

FUNERAL DIRECTOR OR PERSON ACTING AS SUCH (Signature)	FUNERAL DIR. LICENSE NO.	NAME AND ADDRESS OF FACILITY	LICENSE NUMBER (of facility)
21a. *[signature]*	21b.	22a. ███████	22b.
EMBALMER (Signature) 21c. *[signature]*	EMBALMER LICENSE NO. 21d.		

Complete items 23a-c only when certifying physician is not available at time of death to certify cause of death.	To the best of my knowledge, death occurred at the time, date, and place stated. 23a. Signature and Title ▶	LICENSE NUMBER 23b.	DATE SIGNED (Month, Day, Year) 23c.

TIME OF DEATH	DATE PRONOUNCED DEAD (Month, Day, Year)	WAS CASE REFERRED TO MEDICAL EXAMINER/CORONER? (Yes or No)
24. 1:15 A M	25.	26. NO

27. PART I. Enter the diseases, injuries, or complications that caused the death. Do not enter the mode of dying, such as cardiac or respiratory arrest, shock, or heart failure. List only one cause on each line.

		Approximate Interval Between Onset and Death
IMMEDIATE CAUSE (Final disease or condition resulting in death) ➤	a. Ischemic Cardiomyopathy	
	DUE TO (OR AS A CONSEQUENCE OF):	
Sequentially list conditions, if any, leading to immediate cause. Enter UNDERLYING CAUSE (disease or injury that initiated events resulting in death) LAST.	b. Coronary artery disease	
	DUE TO (OR AS A CONSEQUENCE OF):	
	c.	
	DUE TO (OR AS A CONSEQUENCE OF):	

PART II. Other significant conditions contributing to death but not resulting in the underlying cause given in Part I.	AUTOPSY (Yes or No) 28a. NO	IF YES, WERE AUTOPSY FINDINGS CONSIDERED IN DETERMINING CAUSE OF DEATH? (Yes or No) 28b.

29. MANNER OF DEATH	DATE OF INJURY (Month, Day, Year) 30a.	TIME OF INJURY 30b. M	INJURY AT WORK? (Yes or No) 30c.	DESCRIBE HOW INJURY OCCURRED 30d.
☐ Natural ☐ Pending Investigation ☐ Accident ☐ Suicide ☐ Could not be Determined ☐ Homicide	PLACE OF INJURY - Home, Farm, Street, Factory, Office, etc. (Specify) 30e.		LOCATION (Street and Number or Rural Route Number, City or Town, State) 30f.	

CERTIFIER (Check only one)	NAME OF ATTENDING PHYSICIAN IF OTHER THAN CERTIFIER
31. ☒ CERTIFYING PHYSICIAN (Physician certifying cause of death) ☐ MEDICAL EXAMINER ☐ CORONER ☐ PRONOUNCING AND CERTIFYING PHYSICIAN (Physician both pronouncing death and certifying to cause of death)	32.

SIGNATURE AND TITLE OF CERTIFIER To the best of my knowledge, death occurred at the time, date and place, and due to the cause(s) and manner as stated.	LICENSE NUMBER	DATE SIGNED (Month, Day, Year)
33a. ▶ *Dennis Anderson MD*	33b. 9529	33c. 3/1/99

NAME AND ADDRESS OF PERSON WHO SIGNED IN 33a. (Type/Print)
34. DENNIS ANDERSON MD 5146 S DARGAN ST FLORENCE SC 29503

35. ▶ *[signature]*	36. MAR 04, 1999

13

Back Bone Root
* Drawn by Lillian Brown, Freddie's grand-daughter

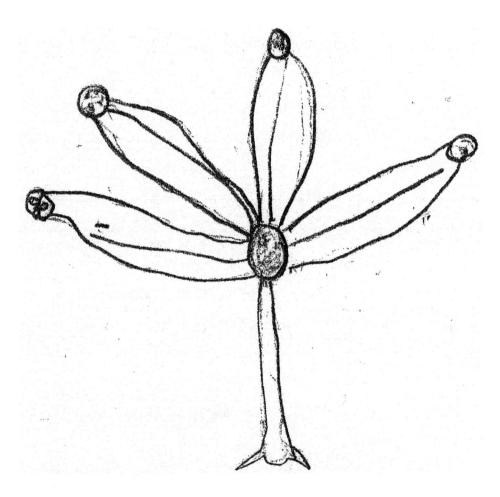

The Sun Flower
*Drawn by Lillian Brown, Freddie's grand-daughter

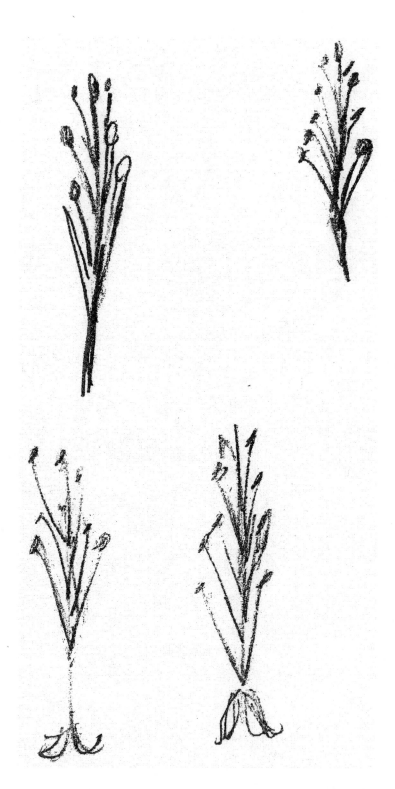

Life Everlasting was good to use when you had the flu.
*Drawn by Lillian Brown, Freddie's grand-daughter

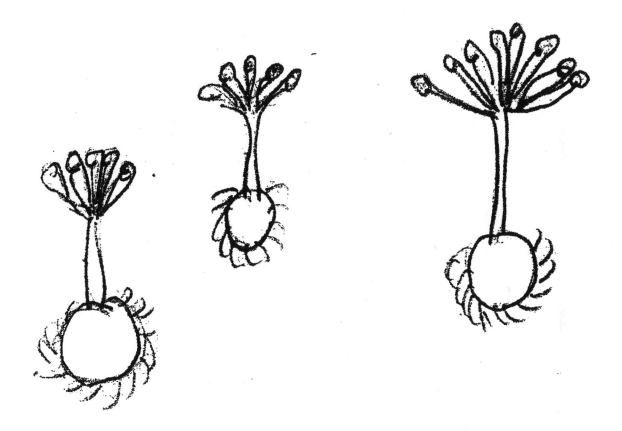

Head Knot was used for slow learners
*Drawn by Lillian Brown, Freddie's grand-daughter

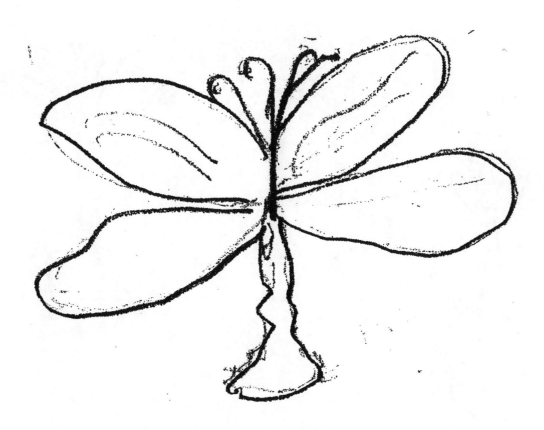

Star Root was used to ease cramps
*Drawn by Lillian Brown, Freddie's grand-daughter

The Organ

My Husband Willis

Anxious, as a teenager to grow up and experience feelings attached to her hormones, Mariah wanted to leave home and start life on her own. The chance came when her mother, Rhinah, recommended that she work for a white family a few miles away ironing, cooking, and cleaning. Mariah said, "I jumped at the opportunity to be on my own." I suppose it's a feeling we've all had once in our lives. How queer is it to talk about leaving home but when we're faced with that moment, how scared we become. Mariah was beautiful and tall. Her posture and her walk were always reflective of royalty. She always wore earrings, necklace, and bracelets when she could get them. Most people put on their clothes first when they wake up in the morning but Mariah had her jewelry on first. Her beauty caught the eyes of Peter Washington, a young tall handsome fellow from Berkeley County, South Carolina. He had the muscles of a lumberjack, and the height of a giant. They both were occupied with the pursuit of pleasure, which produced a son on December 23, 1934. They named him Henry Washington. Mariah eventually took Henry back to Cross, South Carolina. Rhinah and Jippy Brown, her parents were very angry with her for having a baby out of wedlock. Mariah said, "They talked bout me so bad, especially my sister Sibbie." Well you know about sister rivalry. Although disappointed, her parents agreed to keep Henry whom they later referred to as "Growman." He would become a big boy and then a big man. Maybe his physique was a result of the genes from his father, Peter Washington. Rhinah and Jippy loved Dedah Queen enough to let her try again, to make something of herself. This time Mariah went to Edietown, near Kingstree, South Carolina. She heard about another job cleaning, ironing, and cooking for a white family. She would save some money to send home for Henry and her parents. Peter Washington's name would not be mentioned by Mariah for nearly thirty or more years. Several years passed when Mariah caught the eye of another handsome beau' his name was Mandel Anderson. Again, they both were occupied with the pursuit of pleasure that produced a girl on October 12, 1937. They named her Rhinah "Rita" Brown. Still frustrated with her life, Mariah returned home to Cross with an enormous amount of shame. Mariah said "I felt like a fish out of water," trying to explain a second child out of wedlock to my parents. What am I going to do? "I know they aren't going to take care of two children." Little did "Dedah Queen" know, her parents would take the responsibility of raising both Henry and Rhinah in Cross. They truly were parents who did not give up on their daughter. Yes, they were angry and disappointed with Mariah, but they also wanted her to make something of herself. Their support out weighed her doubts. This time before Mariah left home again, her parents prayed that she found a husband and settled down. Mariah found work some forty-five miles away from home. This was the farthest she'd ever been. She heard that they were hiring on the Kennel farm in Cades, South Carolina. The boss would give her a place to stay in exchange for her skills. Mariah ironed, cooked, cleaned and worked in the field for extra money. In 1939,

Mariah met the man of her dreams in Cades. He was a short-built, muscular bow-legged guy. They called him Willis Montgomery. She said, "I met Willis at a church meeting. He looked at me, and when he didn't notice, I would look back at him." This frolicking went on for several more church meetings. Finally, Willis asked her out and they started courting. Willis came from a large family. Sometimes a total of fourteen children and adults would live under one roof at one time (see Willis' family chart). Outside of working in the fields, where they mostly grew cotton, Willis managed a gospel group that traveled from local churches singing. Willis also cut hair on the side. For a man with so many jobs, he was always broke. Their courtship didn't last long because they got married October 26, 1939 in the courthouse of Olanta, South Carolina (see marriage certificate). It was a simple yet eloquent wedding with an abundance of love. They stayed with Willis' family, which added to the fourteen bodies. They had no privacy for their honeymoon, because six to seven people shared one room. Nevertheless, her mother-in-law, Catherine, was able to put up a curtain around their bed giving them some time alone. Everyone would listen to their passionate sounds then tease them the next day. Their passion erupted like a volcano in season, over and over again producing four children and two miscarriages. Mariah always said, "I gave birth to all of my children, on my knees." The midwife would either have Mariah kneel holding either the bedpost or a wooden chair. When the pain became too much to bear, she would squeeze hard into the chair or bedpost. And when the baby was on its way out, the midwife made sure it never touched the floor.

Willis Montgomery's Parents/Siblings

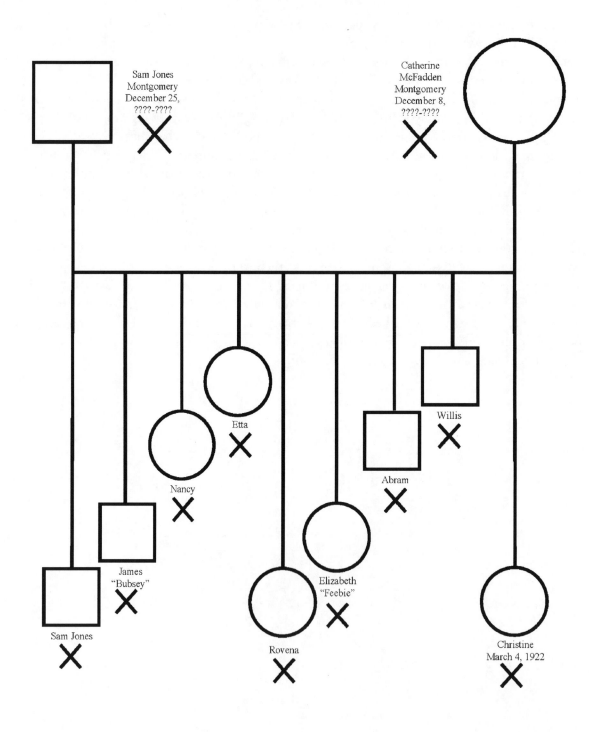

ALL MY CHILDREN

Henry Montgomery was born Henry Brown in Berkeley County of South Carolina. His father's name was Peter Washington of Cross. Henry was born December 23, 1934. He lived with Mariah and Willis when he was about eight years of age. He was a big boy. He attended the public schools of Hebron. Henry accepted Willis as his father figure and became his shadow. He loved his stepfather very much. He changed his name from Henry Brown to Henry Montgomery when he became an adult. He also found his birth father, Peter Washington, and maintained a relationship with him until his recent death.

Rhinah "Rita" Brown was the second child born to Mariah. She was born October 12, 1937 in Berkeley County of South Carolina. She stayed with her grandmother Rhinah in Cross from birth until about the age of ten; however, she would return off and on during her lifetime. Rita would sometimes stay with her mother, Mariah, and stepfather Willis, from time to time. Her life was reminiscent of a child who would constantly move about from one family member to the next, maybe because she missed her mother. I remember Rita saying, "When Mom and Dad (as she would always refer to Willis) worked on Fraley farm in Florence, South Carolina, they sent her to the store and the clerk said I had stolen some candy." Rita denied it. The clerk went to Mariah and Willis and told them that he caught Rita stealing, and they would have to get rid of her or the family would risk remaining on the farm. Rita, with tears in her eyes said, "I did not steal any candy." Mariah and Willis had to make a tough decision that would affect the entire family structure they tried so hard to rebuild. Rita was sent back to Cross to live with cousins. This farm was their only way to make money, and if they had another choice I truly believe they would have made it. Rita later moved to Charleston, South Carolina where she lives today. Her birth father's name is Mandel Anderson and she would one day meet him before his death.

Rita loved her mother Mariah and they would take on some similar characteristics. Mariah gave Rita chances much like her parents gave her, when she messed up. One day while in Cades on the farm, Mariah ran away from Willis and the children because Willis was beating her really severely. The white people she worked for let her stay with them each time when she ran away from Willis. Rita needed a place to stay for she was more of a nomad. She asked her mother for help, but during this time the whites would only allow one colored to stay inside the house. So, Mariah went outside so that her daughter, Rita, could come in and bathe, eat, and rest while she worked the field and stayed in a shanty old farm home dwelling. Rita said the saddest day came when she had to give her mother food out back through a screen door like all the other field help. "My mom sacrificed for me."

Willie Lou Montgomery was my mom. She was born November 3, 1940 during the end of Swing and Bebop music era. She was born on the Kennel farm in Cades, South Carolina. She was Willis and Mariah's first child together. She died at the age of twenty-two years: the reason given was she was having children too fast. Willie Lou had five children and two died; a boy, only a few weeks old, who was delivered by a midwife and was not taken to the hospital immediately thereafter. This created complications, resulting in his death. He was perhaps given a name but no one today is sure what it was. My mom died giving birth to a girl born after me. She was not given a name. Grandmother always said, "Missy (that's what she called her daughter Willie Lou) was having children too fast." Mom had a son before she married my father David Marcus (see Willie Lou's chart). His name is Aaron Montgomery and his father's name was Roosevelt Brockington. He was Aunt Francine's brother, (she would become Henry's first wife). After Willie Lou's death Aaron, her son, would be raised by his grandfather Willis. Willis and Mariah divorced in 1971. The divorce paperwork states the grounds for this separation was that the defendant Mariah Montgomery was guilty of extreme cruelty towards the plaintiff Willis Montgomery (see divorce decree). This was opposite of what Mariah would tell me her grand-daughter.

Anna Jean Montgomery was born September 25, 1942 during World War II. She was the second child born to Willis and Mariah. She is short and stocky like her father. Anna was born in a house outside of New Zion, South Carolina by a midwife. She was a docile child who loved her father very much. She always tried to please him. She is the most generous of all the siblings. Anna has given money and attention to all who ask, and she continues to share with her family. She had one son who died after birth, causes unknown. His name was Laron Montgomery. It was Anna Jean who kept us for six years after our mother Willie Lou died. It took my dad a while to get himself together after losing his young wife of twenty-two. When my father, David Marcus felt better, he sent for us. He told Anna to tell us that we were coming to visit him, when truly we were leaving her to reunite with him. It was a difficult transition, as we cried for Anna. She was perhaps our only mom we first knew.

Lula Mae Montgomery was the third child born to Willis and Mariah. She was born April 10, 1947 on the Kennel farm in Cades. She was the life of a party, and if you were in her presence, you would be laughing right now. She was a true "Aries." Now, one day Lula dared her baby brother "Sonny" to chop off her left pinky finger with an ax. She placed it on a wooden stump and sure enough he chopped it off. A dog grabbed it and ran off. The doctor was unable to reattach the missing pinky, onto her left hand. Sonny was very sorry for what had happened and the family let him have it physically and verbally, even to this day. Lula lived all her adult life with nine fingers, but believe me, she could braid some hair! I know because she used to braid mine.

Willie "Sonny" Montgomery was the baby of the family, born December 5, 1948 on the Kennel farm. Yes, he was the "pinky caper". He never liked the idea of his parents divorcing, even to this day his conversations will often include his disapproval, and he's often resentful to Mariah because of it.

Maria Brown and Willis Montgomery Children

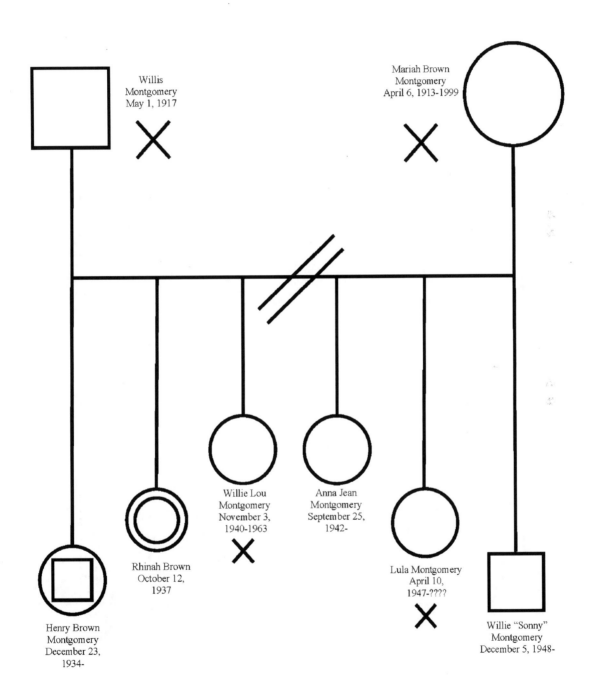

Willis Montgomery May 1, 1917

Mariah Brown Montgomery April 6, 1913-1999

Henry Brown Montgomery December 23, 1934-

Rhinah Brown October 12, 1937

Willie Lou Montgomery November 3, 1940-1963

Anna Jean Montgomery September 25, 1942-

Lula Montgomery April 10, 1947-????

Willie "Sonny" Montgomery December 5, 1948-

Henry Brown Montgomery
and
Francine Brockington Montgomery

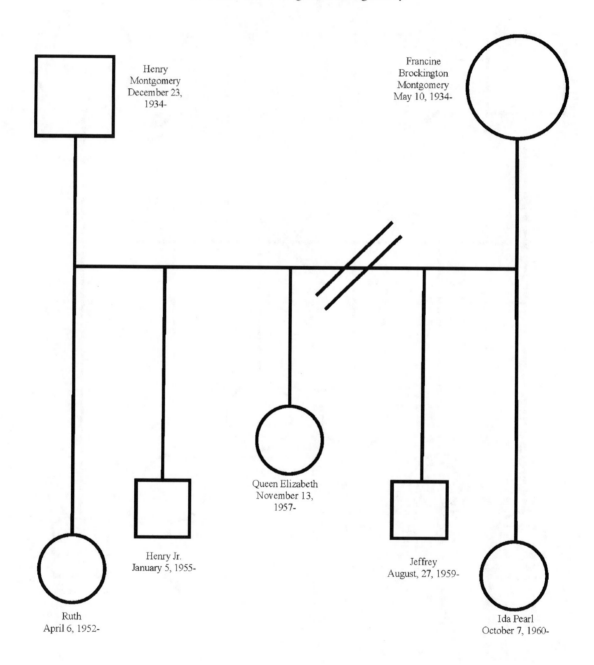

Henry Montgomery December 23, 1934-

Francine Brockington Montgomery May 10, 1934-

Queen Elizabeth November 13, 1957-

Henry Jr. January 5, 1955-

Jeffrey August, 27, 1959-

Ruth April 6, 1952-

Ida Pearl October 7, 1960-

Henry Brown Montgomery
and
Francine Brockington Montgomery
Grandchildren

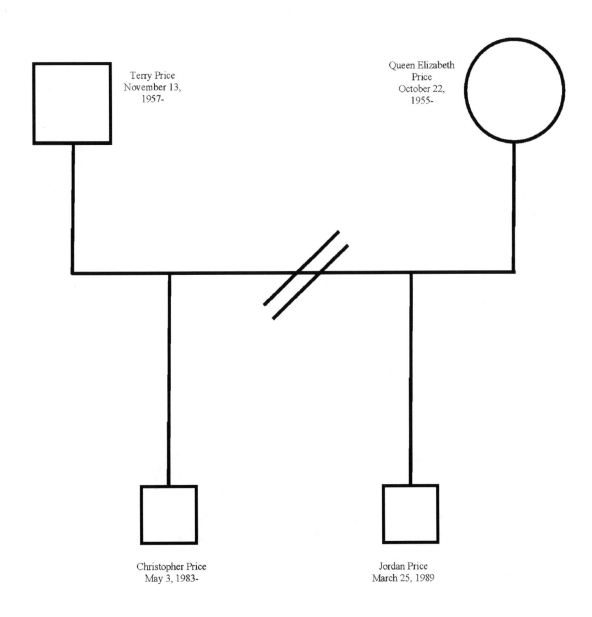

Terry Price
November 13,
1957-

Queen Elizabeth
Price
October 22,
1955-

Christopher Price
May 3, 1983-

Jordan Price
March 25, 1989

Henry Brown Montgomery
and
Francine Brockington Montgomery
Grandchildren

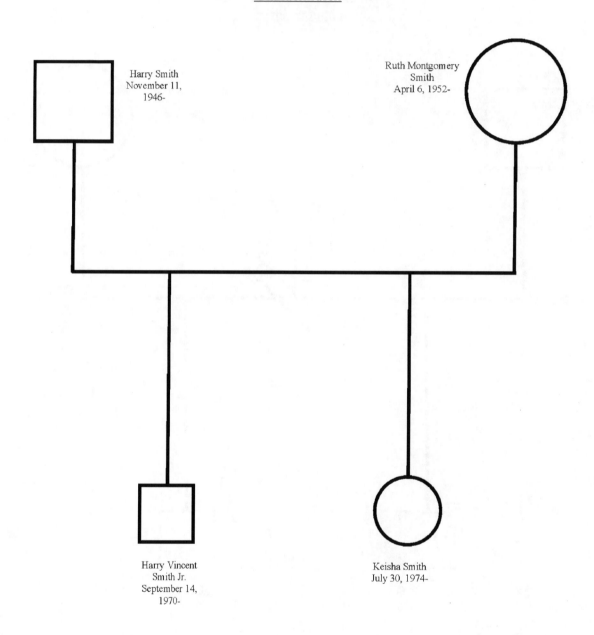

Harry Smith
November 11,
1946-

Ruth Montgomery
Smith
April 6, 1952-

Harry Vincent
Smith Jr.
September 14,
1970-

Keisha Smith
July 30, 1974-

Henry Montgomery and Dorothy Barnes

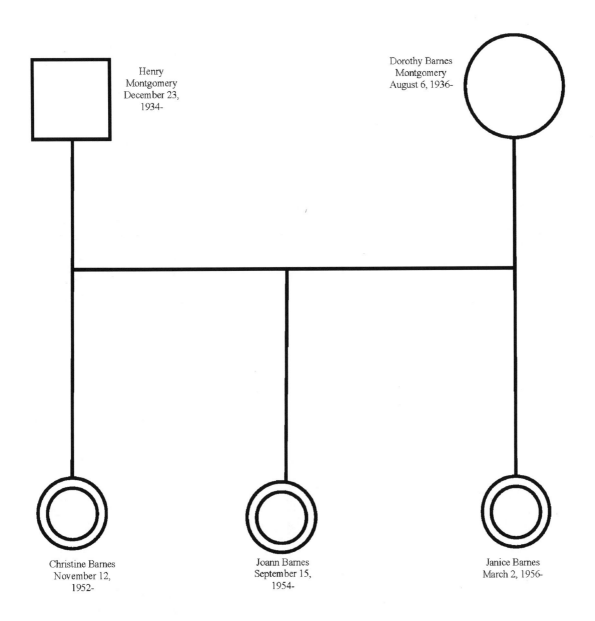

Henry
Montgomery
December 23,
1934-

Dorothy Barnes
Montgomery
August 6, 1936-

Christine Barnes
November 12,
1952-

Joann Barnes
September 15,
1954-

Janice Barnes
March 2, 1956-

Rhina Brown
and
Robert Jamerson

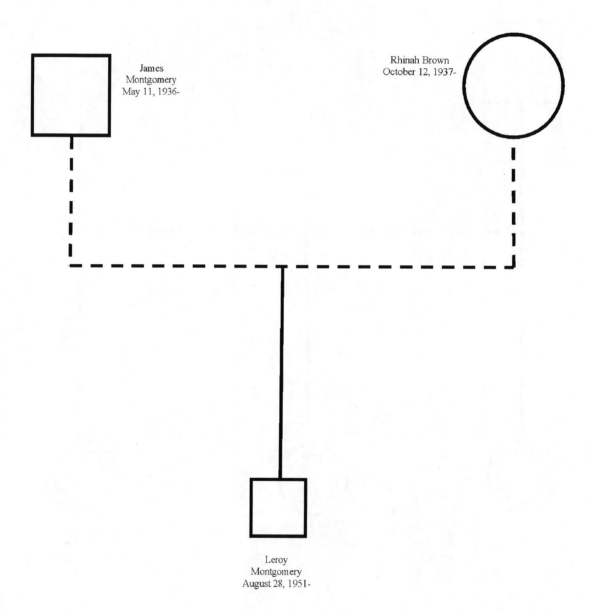

James
Montgomery
May 11, 1936-

Rhinah Brown
October 12, 1937-

Leroy
Montgomery
August 28, 1951-

Rhina Brown and James Montgomery Grandchildren

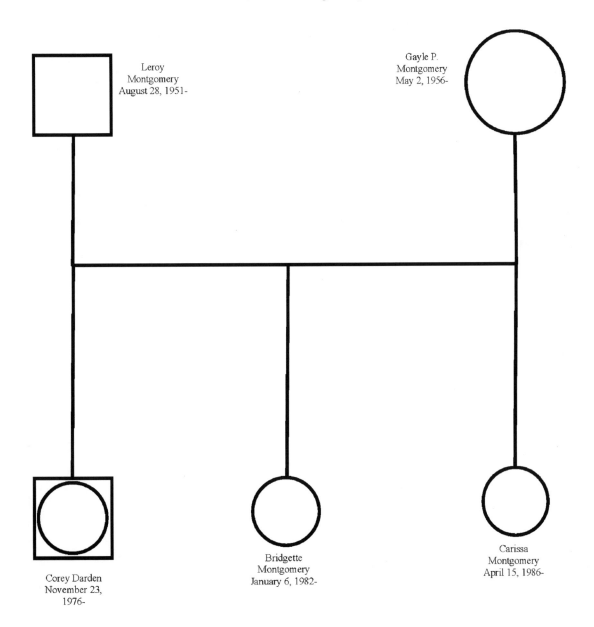

Leroy Montgomery
August 28, 1951-

Gayle P. Montgomery
May 2, 1956-

Corey Darden
November 23, 1976-

Bridgette Montgomery
January 6, 1982-

Carissa Montgomery
April 15, 1986-

Rhina Brown and Robert Jamerson's

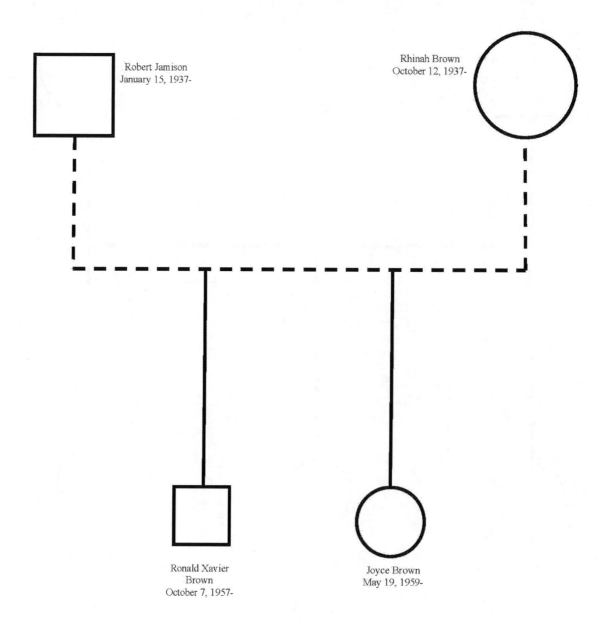

Robert Jamison
January 15, 1937-

Rhinah Brown
October 12, 1937-

Ronald Xavier
Brown
October 7, 1957-

Joyce Brown
May 19, 1959-

Rhina Brown and Robert Jamerson's Grandchildren

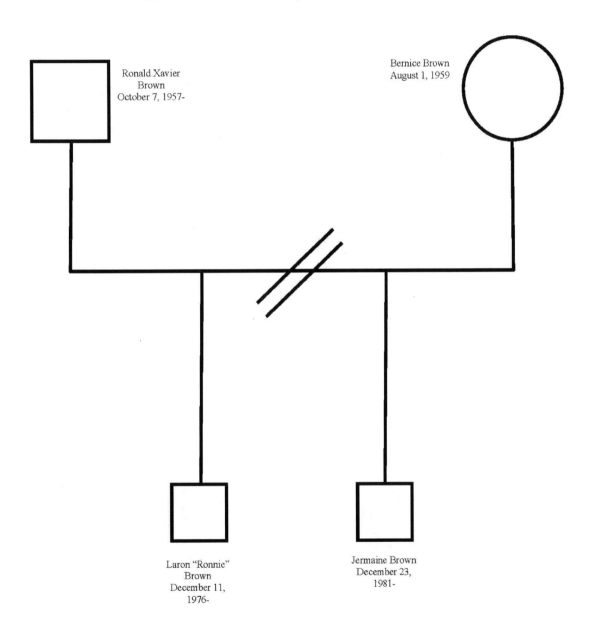

Ronald Xavier
Brown
October 7, 1957-

Bernice Brown
August 1, 1959

Laron "Ronnie"
Brown
December 11,
1976-

Jermaine Brown
December 23,
1981-

Rhina Brown and Robert Jamerson's Grandchildren

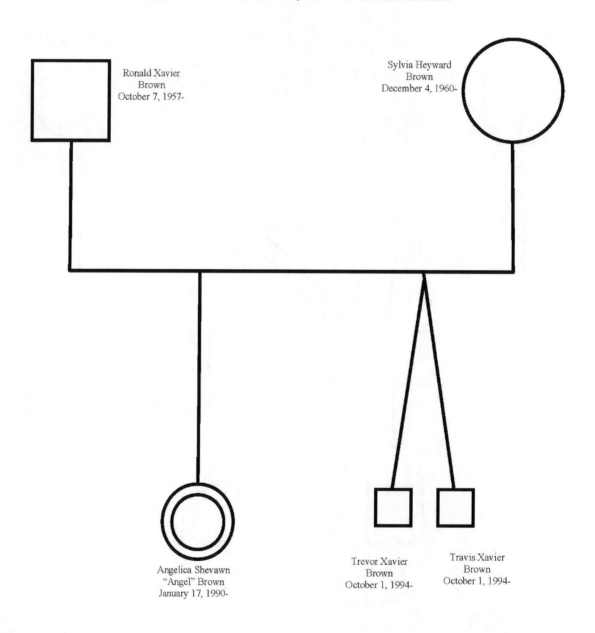

Ronald Xavier
Brown
October 7, 1957-

Sylvia Heyward
Brown
December 4, 1960-

Angelica Shevawn
"Angel" Brown
January 17, 1990-

Trevor Xavier
Brown
October 1, 1994-

Travis Xavier
Brown
October 1, 1994-

Rhina Brown and Robert Jamerson's Grandchildren

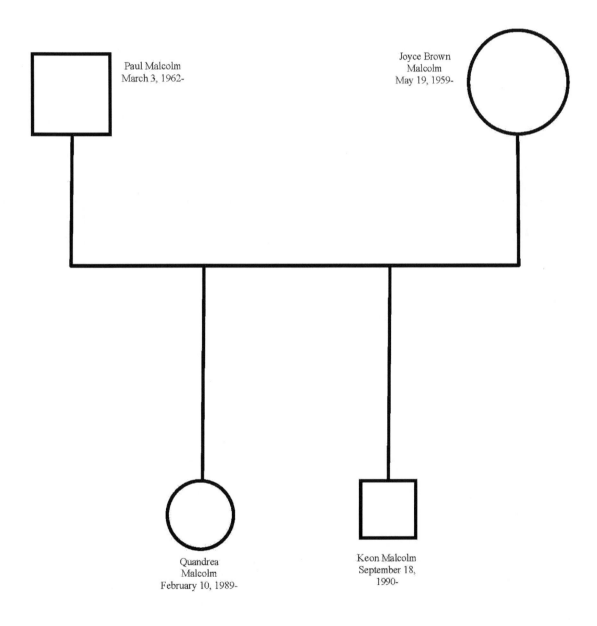

Paul Malcolm
March 3, 1962-

Joyce Brown
Malcolm
May 19, 1959-

Quandrea
Malcolm
February 10, 1989-

Keon Malcolm
September 18,
1990-

Rhina Brown and Luther Green

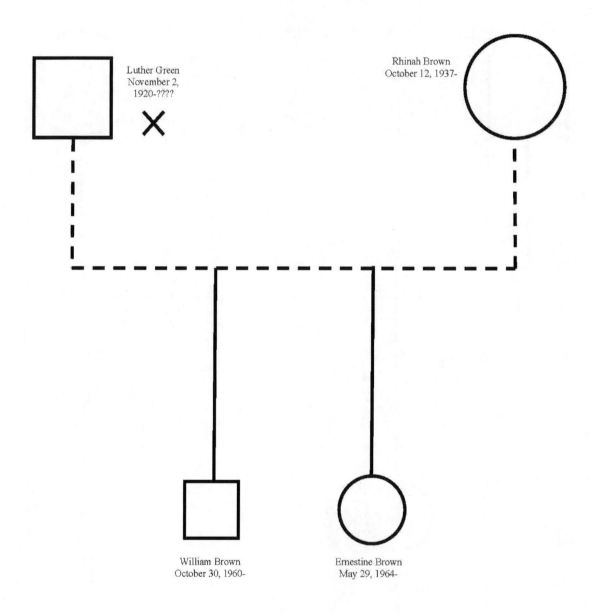

Luther Green
November 2,
1920-????

Rhinah Brown
October 12, 1937-

William Brown
October 30, 1960-

Ernestine Brown
May 29, 1964-

Rhina Brown and Luther Green's Grandchildren

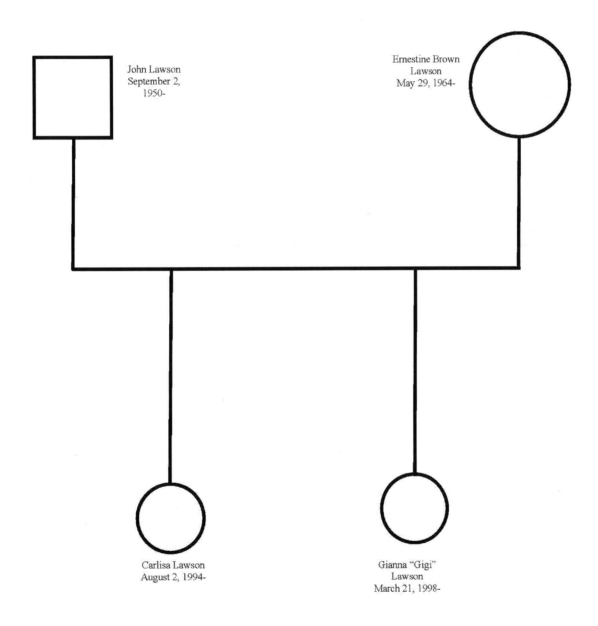

John Lawson
September 2,
1950-

Ernestine Brown
Lawson
May 29, 1964-

Carlisa Lawson
August 2, 1994-

Gianna "Gigi"
Lawson
March 21, 1998-

Rhinah Brown and Luther Green's Grandchildren

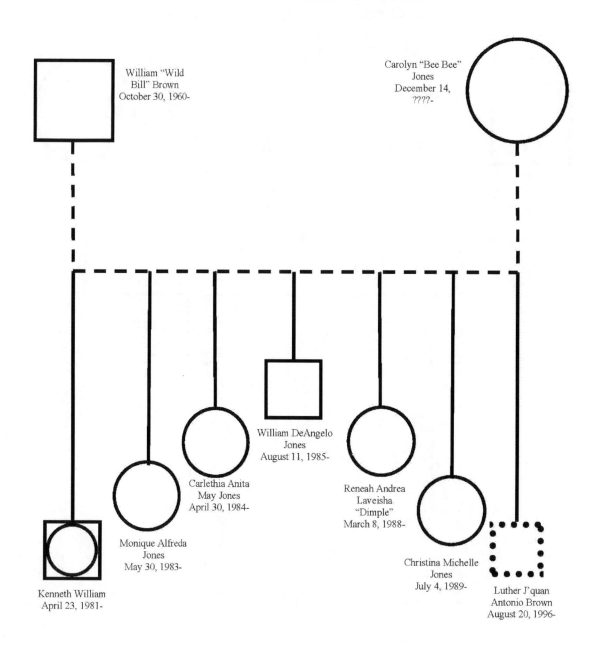

William "Wild Bill" Brown
October 30, 1960-

Carolyn "Bee Bee" Jones
December 14, ????-

Kenneth William
April 23, 1981-

Monique Alfreda Jones
May 30, 1983-

Carlethia Anita May Jones
April 30, 1984-

William DeAngelo Jones
August 11, 1985-

Reneah Andrea Laveisha "Dimple"
March 8, 1988-

Christina Michelle Jones
July 4, 1989-

Luther J'quan Antonio Brown
August 20, 1996-

Willie Lou Montgomery and Roosevelt Borckington

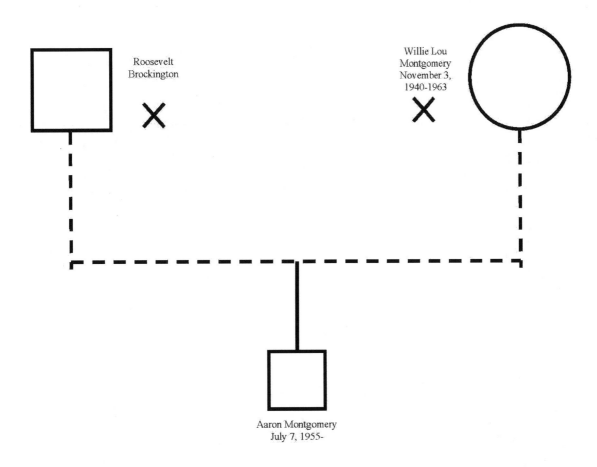

Roosevelt
Brockington

Willie Lou
Montgomery
November 3,
1940-1963

Aaron Montgomery
July 7, 1955-

Willie Lou Montgomery and David Marcus

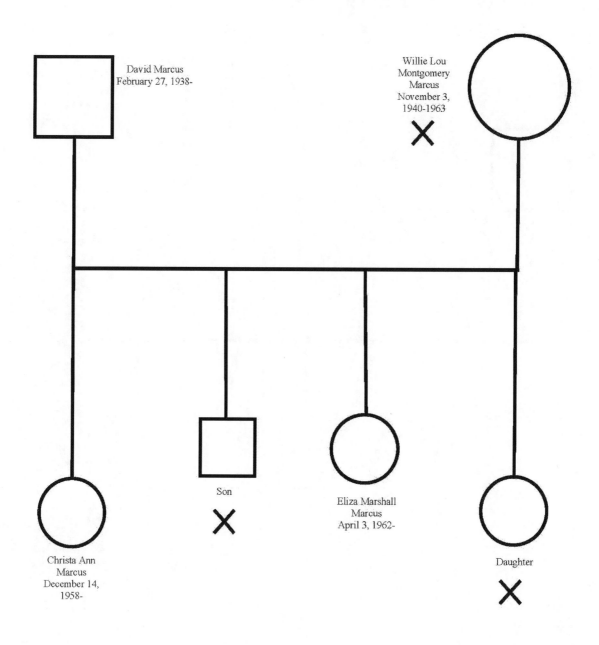

David Marcus
February 27, 1938-

Willie Lou
Montgomery
Marcus
November 3,
1940-1963

Son

Eliza Marshall
Marcus
April 3, 1962-

Christa Ann
Marcus
December 14,
1958-

Daughter

Willie Lou and Roosevelt's Grandchildren

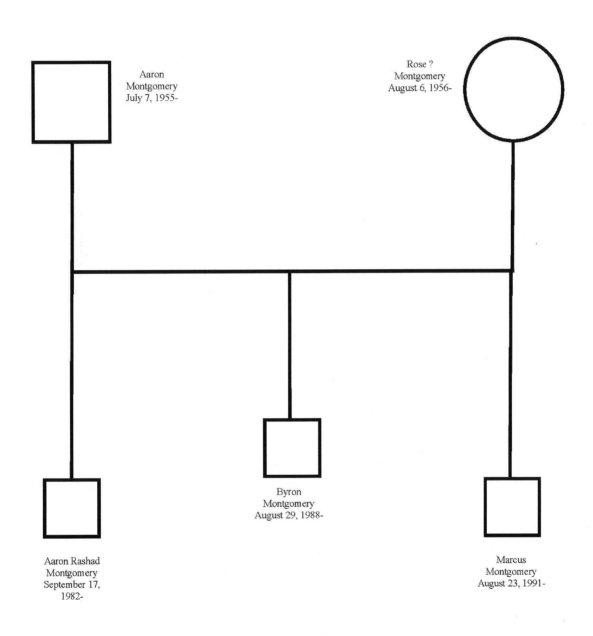

Aaron
Montgomery
July 7, 1955-

Rose ?
Montgomery
August 6, 1956-

Byron
Montgomery
August 29, 1988-

Aaron Rashad
Montgomery
September 17,
1982-

Marcus
Montgomery
August 23, 1991-

Willie Lou and David Marcus' Grandchildren

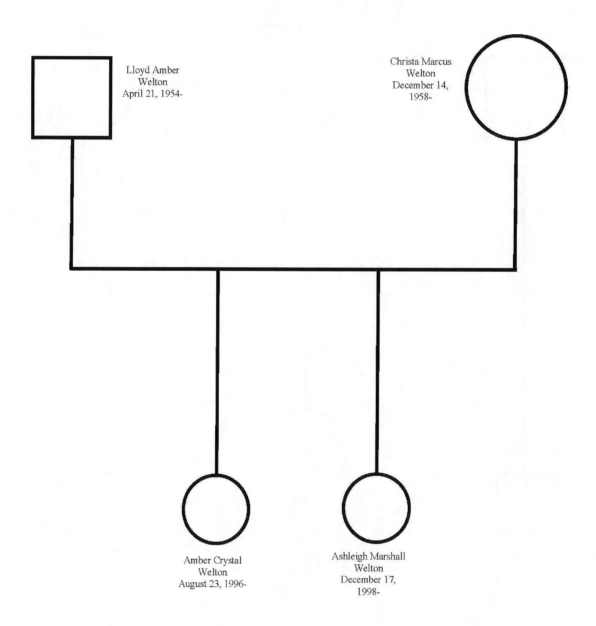

Lloyd Amber
Welton
April 21, 1954-

Christa Marcus
Welton
December 14,
1958-

Amber Crystal
Welton
August 23, 1996-

Ashleigh Marshall
Welton
December 17,
1998-

Willie Lou and David Marcus' Grandchildren

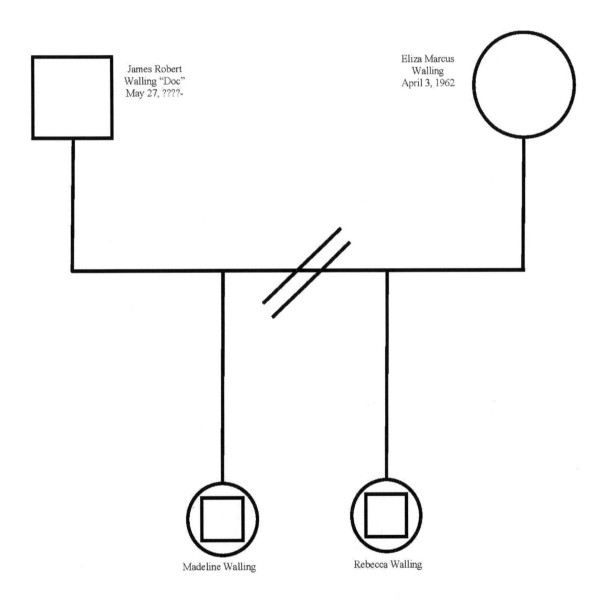

James Robert
Walling "Doc"
May 27, ????-

Eliza Marcus
Walling
April 3, 1962

Madeline Walling

Rebecca Walling

Anna Jean Montgomery and Aaron Green

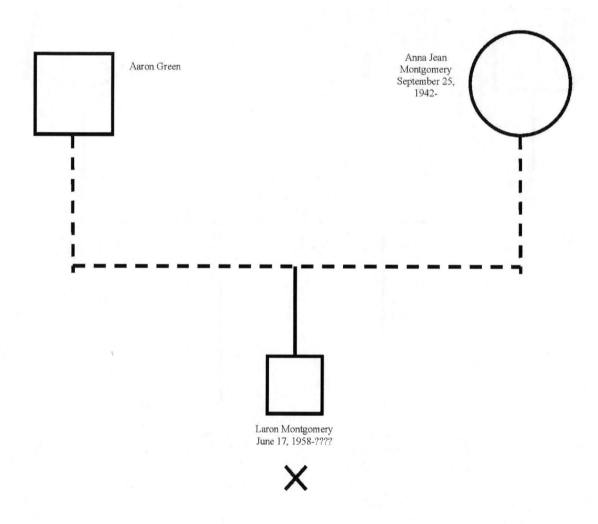

Aaron Green

Anna Jean
Montgomery
September 25,
1942-

Laron Montgomery
June 17, 1958-????

Anna Jean Montgomery and John McFadden

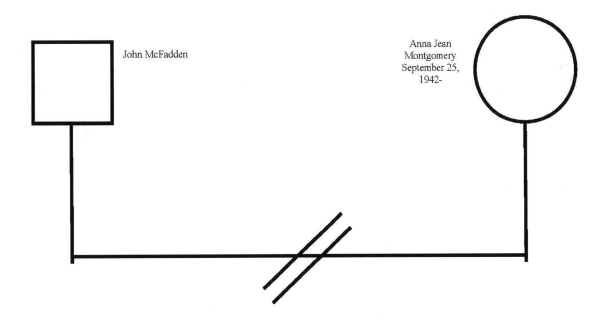

John McFadden

Anna Jean
Montgomery
September 25,
1942-

No Children

Lula Montgomery and Samuel McFadden

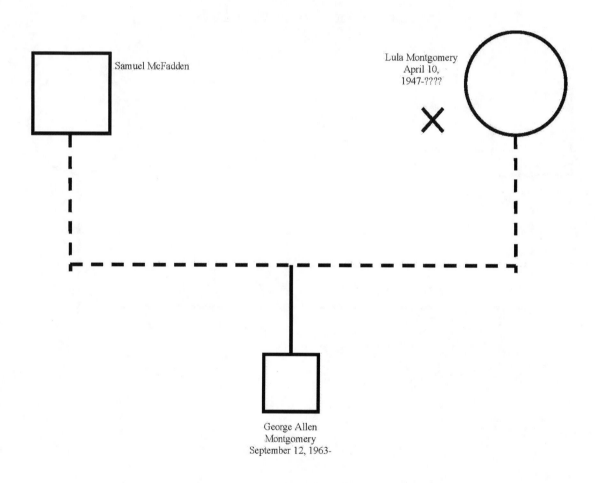

Lula Montgomery and Willie "Son" Dixon

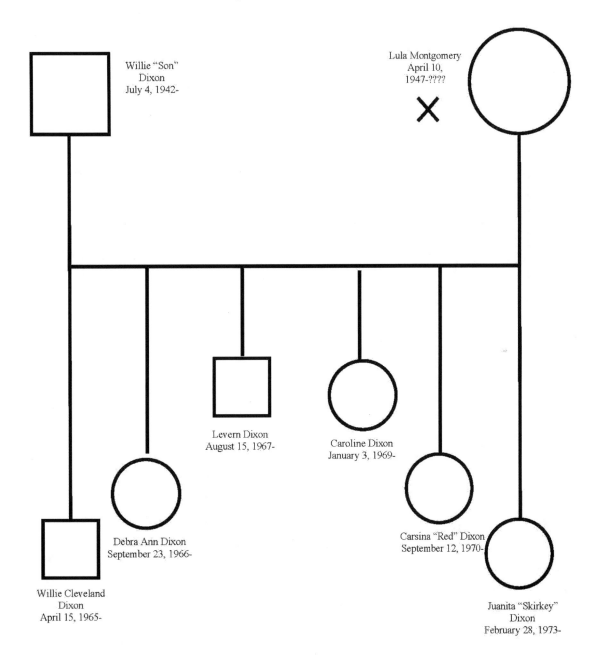

Willie "Son" Dixon
July 4, 1942-

Lula Montgomery
April 10,
1947-????

Levern Dixon
August 15, 1967-

Caroline Dixon
January 3, 1969-

Debra Ann Dixon
September 23, 1966-

Carsina "Red" Dixon
September 12, 1970-

Willie Cleveland
Dixon
April 15, 1965-

Juanita "Skirkey"
Dixon
February 28, 1973-

Lula Dixon and Willie "Son" Dixon Grandchildren

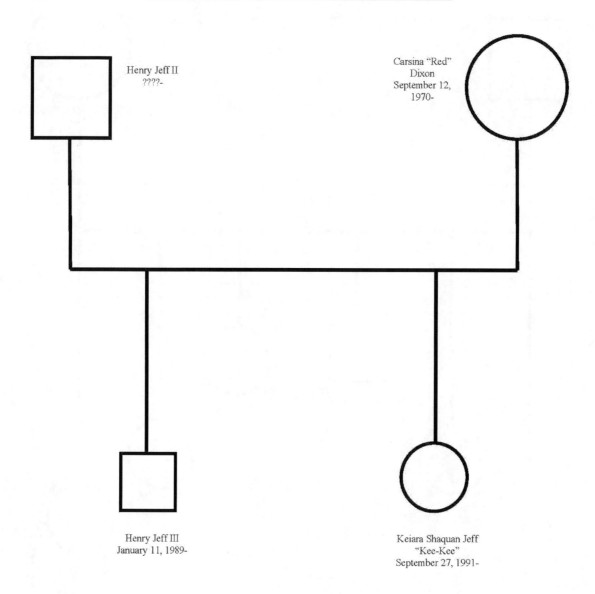

Henry Jeff II
????-

Carsina "Red"
Dixon
September 12,
1970-

Henry Jeff III
January 11, 1989-

Keiara Shaquan Jeff
"Kee-Kee"
September 27, 1991-

Lula Dixon and Willie "Son" Dixon Grandchildren

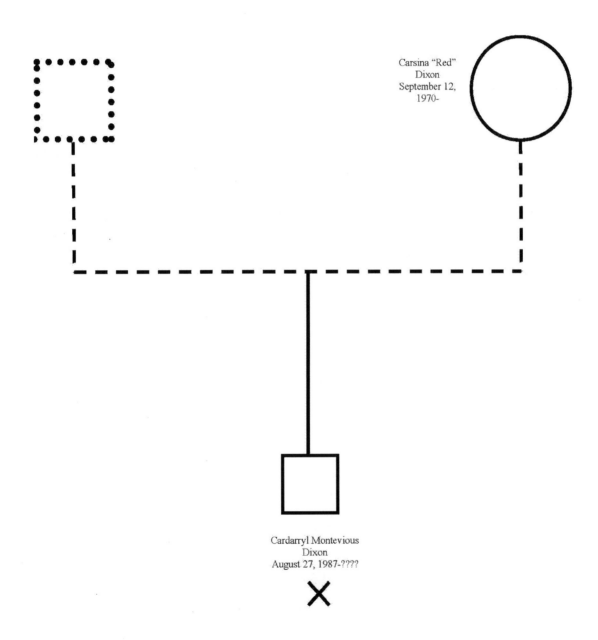

Carsina "Red"
Dixon
September 12,
1970-

Cardarryl Montevious
Dixon
August 27, 1987-????

Lula Dixon and Willie "Son" Dixon Grandchildren

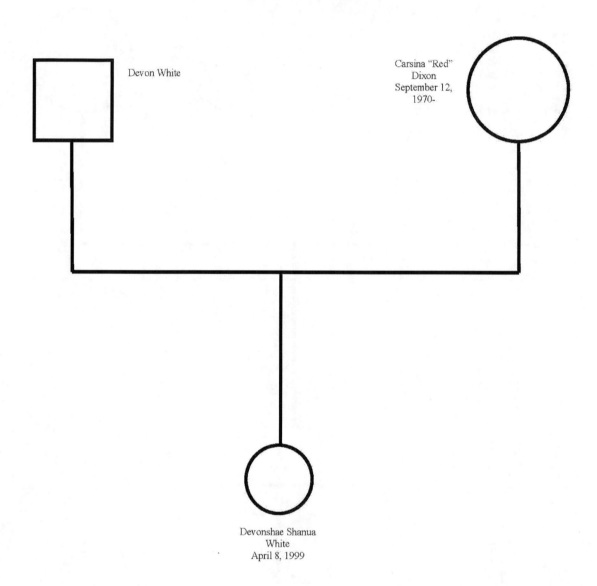

Devon White

Carsina "Red"
Dixon
September 12,
1970-

Devonshae Shanua
White
April 8, 1999

Lula Dixon and Willie "Son" Dixon Grandchildren

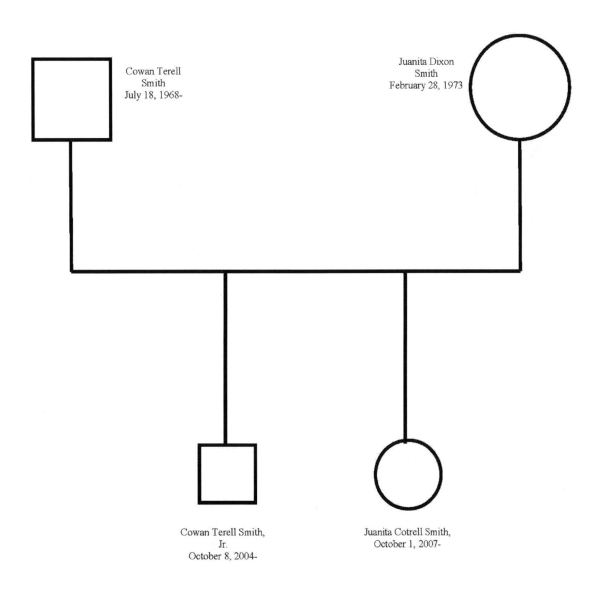

Cowan Terell
Smith
July 18, 1968-

Juanita Dixon
Smith
February 28, 1973

Cowan Terell Smith,
Jr.
October 8, 2004-

Juanita Cotrell Smith,
October 1, 2007-

Willie "Sonny" Montgomery and Jenny R. Pigett

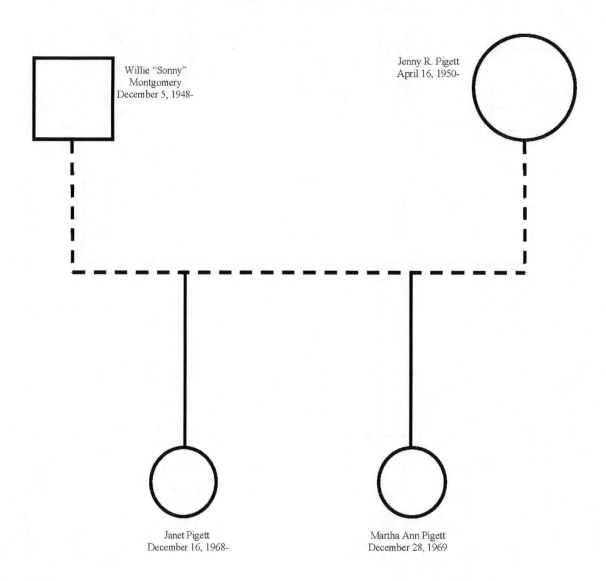

Willie "Sonny"
Montgomery
December 5, 1948-

Jenny R. Pigett
April 16, 1950-

Janet Pigett
December 16, 1968-

Martha Ann Pigett
December 28, 1969

Willie "Sonny" Montgomery and Jenny R. Pigett Grandchildren

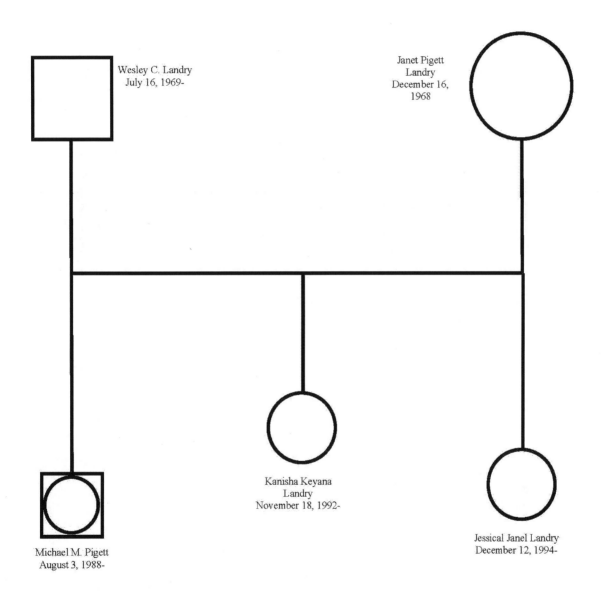

Wesley C. Landry
July 16, 1969-

Janet Pigett
Landry
December 16,
1968

Kanisha Keyana
Landry
November 18, 1992-

Jessical Janel Landry
December 12, 1994-

Michael M. Pigett
August 3, 1988-

Willie "Sonny" Montgomery and Jenny R. Pigett Grandchildren

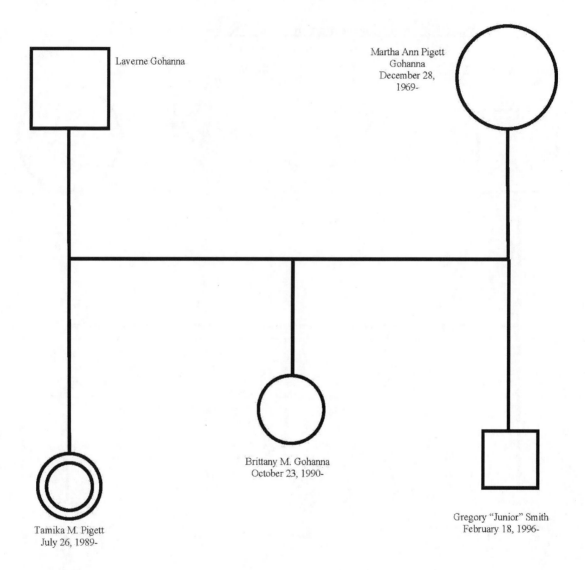

Laverne Gohanna

Martha Ann Pigett
Gohanna
December 28,
1969-

Brittany M. Gohanna
October 23, 1990-

Tamika M. Pigett
July 26, 1989-

Gregory "Junior" Smith
February 18, 1996-

Drawn by Terri Collis
December 31, 2010

Mariah Brown's Parents/Siblings
Jippy Brown-Father
Rhinah Brown-Mother
Children: Mary Brown 1899-1972 Freddie Brown, Sibbie Brown, James Brown,
Mariah Brown-April 6, 1913

Willis Montgomery's Parents/Siblings
Same Jones Montgomery-Father
Catherine Montgomery Mother
Children: Sam Jones Montgomery, James "Bubsey" Montgomery, Nancy Montgomery, Etta
Montgomery, Rovena Montgomery, Elizabeth "Feebie" Montgomery, Abram Montgomery,
Willis Montgomery, and Christine Montgomery

*Mariah Brown and Willis Montgomery Children
Maria Brown Montgomery-Mother born April 6, 1913
Willis Montgomery Father born May 1, 1917
Children: Henry Brown born December 23, 1934, Rhinah Brown born October 12, 1937,
Willie Lou Montgomery born November 3, 1940, Anna Jean Montgomery born September 25,
1942, Lula Montgomery born April 10, 1947, Willie "Sonney" Montgomery, born December
5, 1948.

Henry Brown Montgomery and Francine Brockington Montgomery
Henry Brown Montgomery-Father born December 23, 1934
Francine Brockington Montgomery-Mother born May 10, 1934
Children: Ruth Montgomery born April 6, 1952, Henry Jr. .January 5, 1955, Queen Elizabeth,
November 13, 1957, Jeffery August 27, 1959 and Ida Pearl October 7, 1960.

Henry Brown Montgomery and Francine Brockington Montgomery Grandchildren
Ruth Montgomery Smith-Mother born April 6, 1052
Henry Smith-Father November 11, 1946
Children: Keisha Smith born July 30, 1974 and Henry Vincent Smith, Jr. born September 14,
1970

Henry Brown Montgomery and Francine Brockington Montgomery Grandchildren
Queen Elizabeth Price-mother born November 13, 1957
Terry Price-Father born October 22, 1955
Children: Christopher Price born May 3, 1983 and Jordan Price born March 25, 1989

Henry Montgomery and Dorothy Barnes
Henry Montgomery-Father born December 23, 1934
Dorothy Barnes Montgomery-Mother born August 6, 1934
Children: Christine Barnes, born November 12, 1952, Janice Barnes born March 2, 1956, and
Joann Barnes born September 15, 1954.

Rhinah Brown and James Montgomery
Rhinah Brown-Mother born October 12, 1937
James Montgomery-Father born May 11, 1936
Children: Leroy Montgomery born August 28, 1951

Rhinah Brown and Robert Jamison
Rhinah Brown-Mother born October 12, 1937
Robert Jamison-Father born January 15, 1937
Children: Ronald Xavier Brown, born October 7, 1957 and Joyce Brown born May 19, 1959.

Rhinah Brown and Luther Green
Rhinah Brown-Mother born October 12, 1937
Luther Green-Father born November 2, 1920
Children: William Brown, born October 30, 1960 and Ernestine Brown born May 29, 1964

Rhinah Brown and James Montgomery Grandchildren
Leroy Montgomery-Father born August 28, 1951
Gayle Montgomery, born May 2, 1951
Children: Corey Darden, born November 23, 1976, Bridgette Montgomery, born January 6, 1982, and Carissa Montgomery, born April 15, 1986.

Rhinah and Robert Jamison Grandchildren
Ronald Xavier Brown-Father born October 7, 1957
Berniece Brown-Mother August 1, 1959
Children: Laron "Ronnie" Brown born December 11, 1976 and Jermaine Brown, born December 23, 1981.

Rhinah and Robert Jamison Grandchildren
Ronald X. Brown-Father born October 7, 1957
Sylvia Heyward-Brown-Mother December 4, 1960
Children: Angrizea Brown born January 17, 1990, Trevor Brown born October 2, 1994 and Travis Xzavier born October 2, 1994

Rhinah Brown and Robert Jamison Grandchildren
Joyce Brown Malcolm-Mother, May 19, 1959
Paul Malcolm-Father born March 13, 1962
Children: Quandrea Malcolm born February 10, 1989 and Keon Malcolm born September 15, 1990.

Rhinah Brown and Luther Green Grandchildren
Ernestine Brown Lawson-Mother born May 29, 1964
John Lawson-Father born September 2, 1950
Children: Carlisa Lawson born August 2, 1994 and Gianna "Gigi" Lawson born March 21, 1998.

Rhinah Brown and Luther Green Grandchildren
William "Wild Bill" Brown, born October 30, 1960
Carolyn "Bee Bee" Jones, born December 14, __?
Children: Kenneth William born April 23, 1981, Monique Alfreda Jones, born May 30, 1983, Carlethia Anita Jones, born April 30, 1984, William DeAngelo Jones, born August 11,. 1985, Reneah, Andrea Laveisha "Dimple" Jones, born March 8, 1988, Christina Michelle Jones, born July 4, 1989 and Luther J'quan Antonio Brown, born August 20, 1996.

Willie Lou Montgomery and Roosevelt Brockingtons' Child
Willie Lou Montgomery-Mother, born November 3, 1940
Roosevelt Brockington-Father DOB?
Child: Aaron Montgomery, born July 7, 1955

Willie Lou Montgomery and David Marcus children
Willie Lou Marcus-Mother, born November 3, 1940
David Marcus-Father, born February 27, 1938
Children: Christa A. Marcus born December 14, 1958 and Eliza Marshell Marcus born April 3, 1962.

Willie Lou and Roosevelt Grandchildren
Aaron Montogmery-Father born July 7, 1955
Rose Marie Montgomery-Mother, born August 6, 1956
Children: Aaron Rashad Montgomery born September 17, 1982, Byron Montgomery born August 29, 1988 and Marcus Montgomery born August 23, 1991.

Willie Lou and David Marcus Grandchildren
Christa Marcus Welton-Mother born December 14, 1958
Lloyd Welton Father-born April 21, 1956
Children: Amber Crystal Welton born August 23, 1996 and Ashleigh Marshell Welton, born December 17, 1998

Willie Lou and David Marcus Grandchildren
Eliza Marcus-Mother, born April 3, 1962
James Robert "Doc" Walling May 27?
Children: Madeline Walling born October 27 ? and Rebecca Walling born March 12 ?

Anna Jean Montgomery and Aaron Green
Anna Jean Montgomery, mother born September 25, 1942
Aaron Green-Father, DOB
Children: Laron Montgomery, born June 17, 1958

Anna Jean and John McFadden
Anna Jean Montgomery, Mother, born September 25, 1942
John McFadden-Father, DOB
Children: None

Lula Montgomery and Samuel McFadden Children
Lula Montgomery-Mother, born April 10, 1947
Samuel McFadden DOB
Children: George Allen Montgomery, born September 12, 1963

Lula Montgomery and Willie "Son" Dixon
Lula Dixon-Mother, born April 10, 1947
Willie "Son" Dixon, Father born July 4, 1942
Children: Willie Cleveland Dixon, born April 15, 1965, Debra Ann Dixon born September 23, 1967, Levern Dixon, born August 15, 1968, Caroline Dixon, born January 3, 1969, Carsina "Red" Dixon, born September 12, 1970, Juanita "Skirkey" Dixon, born February 28, 1973.

Lula Dixon and Willie Dixon Grandchildren
Carsina "Red" Dixon-Mother born September 23, 1970
Father,Unknown
Children: Cadarryl Montevious Dixon, born August 27, 1987

Lula Dixon and Willie Dixon Grandchildren
Carsina Dixon-Mother, born September 12, 1970
Father: Henry Jeff II DOB
Children: Henry Jeff,III, born January II, 1989, and Keiara Shquan Jeff born Septenber 27, 1991

Lula Dixon and Willie Dixon Grandchildren
Carsina Dixon Mother, born September 12, 1970
Devon White-Father DOB
Children Devonshae Shanua White, born April 8, 1999

Willie "Sonny" Montgomery and Jenny R. Pigett children
Willie Montgomery, Father born December 5, 1948
Jenny R Pigett, Mother, born April 16, 1950
Children: Janet Pigett born December 16, 1968 and Martha Ann Pigett born December 28, 1969

Willie "Sonny" Montgomery and Jenny R. Pigett grandchildren
Janet Pigett Landry Mother born December 12, 1968
Wesley Landry, father born July 16, 1967
Children: Michael M. Pigett, born August 3, 1988, Kanisha Keyana Landry born November 18, 1992 and Jessixca Janel Landry born December 12, 1994.

Willie "Sonny" Montgomery and Jenny R. Pigett grandchildren
Martha A. Pigett Gohanna Mother, born December 28, 1969
Laverne Gohanna DUB
Children: Tarneka M. Pigett born November 26, 1989, Brittany M. Gohanna born October 23, 1990, and Gregory "Juniior" Smith born February 18, 1996.

Florence, South Carolina

Grandmother promised her daughter Willie Lou that she would take care of her girls Christa and Eliza however, David Marcus our father also wanted us. Knowing the value of a promise on one's deathbed, my father allowed us to stay with our Grandma during the week to go to school in the city. He picked us up every Friday after school and we returned Monday mornings. My father, David Marcus grew tobacco in the summer so we stayed with him for the entire summer months from June to August. Grandmother and Daddy raised us and, they shared in the responsibilities equally.

Grandmother cleaned houses when she moved to Florence. I recall her saying that some employers were good to her and others were "nasty." I remember one employer in particular named Mrs. McCloud. She was a widow, and she lived in a huge house with several servants, and grandma was the one who ironed, cleaned, and cooked. Grandma did not like this lady and you could hear it in her voice when she returned home every day. She would say that Mrs. McCloud would talk to her with no respect as an adult. Grandma would call her "nasty." On the other hand, I remember Grandma speaking nicely about one employer named Mrs. Hyman. She was the wife of a dentist. Grandma called her "little bird," because of her physique. "Little bird" would pick Grandma up early in the morning just as the clouds broke away from the night's darkness. Grandma would return late in the evening, as the darkness in the sky took away the puffy shadows that lingered all through the day. My sister Christa and I would always be so happy to see Grandma return home from work; we were almost like dogs who greet their owners with unbridled joy. At one point, we even wrote a song about "Little bird," which was complimentary to her character. Mrs. Hyman would give us old clothes she couldn't wear anymore. We would always accept them and pick out things we would wear, and throw away the others or make scrap rags out of them. One time when "Little bird," gave us a load of clothes, this time, we found a pair of flat pointed toe mustard colored shoes. The toe area hurt my sister's feet, I thought because she has bunions; she gave them to me. I liked them, but the toe hurt my feet as well. One day, I decided to look inside the toe of the shoes and found a twenty-dollar bill folded in the point of one of the shoes. I was very happy. I couldn't believe I had $20 to myself. From then on, we checked pockets and shoes of all the clothes "Little bird," gave us.

Grandmother lived on the property of Mrs. Elizabeth Lee and her daughter, Ruby, and son-in-law, Mr. McKinley Godbolt. They had three children: Butch, Michael, and Melissa; they were all around our age. We lived in a stone house we rented from Mrs. Lee in the early 1970s. It had no running water, no bathroom and no central heat or air. We had a water pump in the backyard, and an "out house." We had two wood stoves: one in the kitchen and the other in the dining room. This house was all my grandmother could afford. She was starting over after her divorce from Willis. Grandma's weekly income was $25 working for Mrs. Hyman which include

59

the duties of washing, ironing, cooking and cleaning. Sometimes she had to clean the house and cook for the same amount of money. Grandma ironed shirts so well until her employers couldn't believe they weren't sent out to the cleaners. Grandma would always tell us, "don't spend to your last dime, always save a piece of money back." I still can't figure out how she paid rent, house bills, bought groceries, took care of us, and put some money aside.

The Old House

On the front porch, you will find Christa Marcus and Eliza M. Marcus enjoying a summers'
day. Christa is sitting on the porch and Eliza is sitting on the bench.

The Old House

The outside of the old house was made out of stone, and it had no paint (see previous picture). It had two front doors because it could be used as a two family apartment; nevertheless, we used it as a single family home. From the left front side of the house you would enter grandmother's bedroom. It had a bed and dresser, none of which matched. We banged nails in the wall to hang up clothes on hangers. The next room was the guest bedroom. It had no doors, so Grandmother hung up a thick bedspread by banging it with nails in the wall; this was same method her mother-in-law Catherine, used on her honeymoon. She attached a clothes-line to the spread and ran it from one end of the wall to the next. The ends would be wrapped and tied around a nail in the wall. The final room on the left side was our bedroom: Christa and Marshell. Our bed sagged in the middle of it so badly we ended up in the center pushing each other away all during the night. I shared a bed and bedroom with my sister as long as I can remember growing up. Our room had a window on the back wall and a side back door was used to exit, outside the house. We had electricity in the old stone house. Grandma attached a string from the chain of the ceiling light to the bedpost, making it easy for us to cut the light off without getting up. This was like a modern-day "clapper." You've seen the commercial when the old lady gets into bed and claps her hands and the light goes out: it has some sort of built-in sensor I suppose. From the back door of our room, you could see the back porch of Mrs. Lee's house and the clothes-line. Mrs. Lee was very old but she was still active. She was thin with long gray hair that she wore in two big braids. Her voice was quiet even when she raised it and it was still but a whisper. She was an educated African American woman and always had some good advice for her grandchildren, daughter and even us (Christa and Marshell). In the yard was an old tree that appeared to have been struck by lightning and an old car parked nearby that often marked our property line. It was an old light blue car that was apparently broken down and used for parts. The metal would bend easily as we jumped on the old car. We made a lot of noise jumping on that old car, but no one seemed to care or mind.

Grandma washed clothes at night around 11:00 pm. I know that seems late but remember Grandmother got home from work around 8:00 or 9:00 p.m. She had to cook and rest for a few minutes before we'd wash clothes in a big black "wash pot." It was round at the base, like a cooking pot. We put wood all around it that blazed into fire when ignited. The water in the wash pot would boil, then Grandma would add, "lye soap." After washing the white clothes we would start the procedure over for the dark clothes. We turn on the porch lights on because we had to see the clothes line and the water pump which were opposite each other. Grandma had a long stick to stir the clothes as if to cook a stew. The clothes would stay in the pot until Grandma thought they were clean. Once the clothes had boiled enough, we would take the big stick and dip them out and put them into a tub of cold water to be rinsed. We had to let the boiled clothes sit in the cold water for a while before we could tolerate the heat on our hands. After several loads of clothes came out of the boiling pot and put into the rinse water, the rinse water would eventually became hot, then we would have to add some more cold water from the water pump. We tried to twist most of the water out of the clothes before hanging them on the clothes line. I remember Elvis Presley was on television one night during our routine clothes washing night. Yes, we had an old thirteen inch black and white television. Well, Elvis beach party movie was on and Christa and I would run in and out from the clothes-line to the Television set trying to do two things at once. Grandma fussed at us by saying, "You better mind how you run in and out!" all the while waving her "spanking stick" at us." Yet, she always allowed us to get a sneak peek of Elvis Presley twisting his hips and when we would squeal, she would wail in a good laugh as she moved her head back and forth while patting her knees.

A view of the right side of the old stone house would take you into the living room; this was the cleanest room inside. It was arranged with many artificial flowers because Grandma liked them best. She said, "They last forever." There was a record player with an eight track tape deck. We had records and albums of Michael Jackson: "I'm going back to Indiana," "Rockin Robin," and "ABC," along with some gospel singers. There were assorted sofas and chairs that did not match. There was a picture of Jesus Christ that lit up when you plugged it up and a Bible on the table on a knitted doily. The next room was the dining room. It had a wood heater, a wood box and chairs with no table. The soot on the walls came from the old wood heater. The smell of soot throughout the house lasted the entire year. Sometimes we would paint the walls to keep them clean. We would hold our plates in our laps snuggle around the heater in the cold of winter to eat. Someone would always kick over their milk by mistake. Grandma always made a bet as to who it would be each night. Finally, the kitchen was next. It had a wood stove with four eyes, a counter and perhaps shelves. This was the darkest of all the rooms, maybe because the sun didn't shine on this side of the house. There was a door that led outside from the kitchen, where you could see the water pump, and the deep ditch. Around the corner to the left of the ditch was the "out house." I was always afraid to go inside because it was cold and scary, plus it smelled. We took a good long bath once a week, usually Saturday night just before Sunday, in a big bath tub. This tub was made out of metal and had two metal handles on each side. It was placed inside near the heater in the cold of winter however it could only hold one person at a time. Otherwise, we took sponge baths nightly in the "foot tub" (a small metal with two handles). We also had a basin for morning touch ups and to brush our teeth. The water was then poured into the deep ditch. Grandma would also keep a "night pot" in the house to serve as an, over-night latrine in case someone had to use it. It would be dumped early the next morning in the "out house" or the ditch.

Several years later, Grandma moved to theOakland Heights Apartments a newly developed community being built all around the old stone house. Grandma was the first tenant (see document). I was in the seventh grade when I took my first bath in a real tub with running water. It was the first time we had a kitchen sink to wash dishes. And we no longer had to go outside to the "out house." We were so thankful we told Grandma that we would wash dishes every day without her ever asking us. She said, "I won't let you forget it." And she didn't either!

Grandma didn't drive, never did from my understanding, so she bought a brand new red wagon. We used this wagon to carry our clothes to and from the washerette, grocery store and many other nearby places she could think of. We had to walk about a fourth of a mile to the nearest washerette, because the one in the apartments had not been built yet. Oakland Heights was on Oakland Avenue, a busy and well-known street in Florence, South Carolina. We were so happy to be at a washerette and not boiling clothes in the yard. We even had the opportunity to watch Elvis beach parties without any interruptions. Mrs. Chris store was the closest. She was the white lady with whom my grandmother traded (bought groceries from). Mrs. Horne was the black store owner across the Street, whom we would go to every now and then. But most people gravitated to Mrs. Chris store. Mrs. Chris was fair and treated everybody with respect; we even got to know her entire family. She stayed in business until she retired. She sold her store many years later; however, it is still in operation, with new owners, even more than thirty years later.

In the summer, we would walk downtown, of course, without the wagon. We used to love KRESS. This was a dime store where you could buy almost anything for a buck. They had the best hot dogs in town. We would get our Easter dresses from downtown, and do Christmas shopping and other occasional shopping here. Grandma used to go to "Millers M System" a well-known grocery store downtown Dargan street in Florence, to get her meats when Mrs. Chris' store didn't have what she wanted. I observed my first music store downtown. It was called Summerall Music, and they sold pianos and sheet music. As I was looking through the window one day, the owner came outside and invited me inside. I told him that I could play the piano a little so he asked me to play for him. I played a simple C major scale with both hands. The music clerk then gave me a piece of sheet music written by Dottie Rambo and said, "One day you will be able to play this and many songs." I treasured that music like an Olympic finalist would treasure his medals. I still have it today, but the music store is gone. I wish I had a chance to thank that store clerk. Mr. Lonnie Crews known as "Motor Rooster" owned a black music shop. Mr. "Rooster" had a favorite saying, "If there's another rooster, it must be a phony." In his shop he had gospel music, rock and roll, eight-track tapes, records, albums and many collectibles. He also took pictures in the back, group or individual. His wife Mrs. Hattie Crews had a beauty salon next door. Mr. Rooster even had his own television show called, "The Motor Rooster Show." It was in the same format as "Soul Train," but local kids did the dancing. It was exciting to see black people on television.

The Journey to New Zion, South Carolina

Mariah Montgomery attended the Howard Chapel African Methodist Episcopal (AME) Church in New Zion, South Carolina. This is where her sister-in-law Christine Montgomery, was from. The funniest thing about Mariah's divorce was that all of her in-laws kept a relationship with her as if she was still married to Willis. Now, that's saying something very admirable about her character and personality. We started our journey each first Sunday morning with a ride in Aunt Etta Burgess, white Ford car. This was Grandma's other sister-in-law (see Willis family chart). Now, Etta was short and very particular about things. She was neat, and she didn't throw away much. She was well versed in the polities of the African Methodist Episcopal Church. She loved her church and she was a faithful member. Aunt Etta was single without any children. Grandmother said she had a baby but every time she had visitors come by, she would always make them keep extremely quiet. Grandmother said the baby died in its' sleep. Ever since then, Aunt Etta put her energy into the church and her music. She picked on the piano with one finger on each hand with open chords (several octaves apart). All in all, she was a dedicated musician as she always kept a steady tempo and melody going. Aunt Etta had a white straight drive Ford car, and boy could she lay down on the clutch to change the gears; these were in the steering wheel. You could almost walk along side the car during the process. Aunt Etta didn't have power steering and it took a while to make a turn. Each first Sunday morning, Aunt Etta, Grandma, Christa, and myself, were going to Howard Chapel church in New Zion; while Aunt Etta attended St. John AME in New Zion. Her pastor was the Rev. Bert Robinson, whom she really liked. You could tell by the way she spoke of him to others, as well as all the extra responsibilities she took on at the church. She often attended afternoon programs even though she lived in Florence, South Carolina some forty miles away. She always made sure the pastor was comfortable and well fed, as she would prepare food every Sunday. You could pop her car trunk and there would be an entire meal of fried chicken, green beans, rice and pound cake. They say the best way to a man's heart is through his stomach. She would have been the perfect preacher's wife; however, I think he was married. The ride to New Zion offered a view of the countryside. Houses were sporadically situated off the roadside, and many were made of wood or brick. My sister Christa would play a game by calling out which house we liked the most. It seemed our eyes never left the car window, as we noticed everything along the way. We remember seeing stores and people standing in front of clubs later on, this scenery would become a reason for which to return to New Zion. We would arrive at Aunt Christine's house early enough to change clothes and be at church by 11:00 a.m.. Christine and Etta were sisters and Willis was their brother (see Willis's family chart). Christine was blind. Grandma said the Lord took Christine's sight because she was living a sinful life, and to get her attention, He took her sight." Neither story would ever give Christine back her sight in both eyes, but she adjusted her life without sight and was very successful at it.

She was the first blind person I'd ever seen who could count coin money. She would feel along the outside edge of the coin with her fingers to determine if it was smooth like a penny or nickel or a rough texture of a dime or quarter. I thought it was magic that she was able to give correct change. Many of Aunt Christine's houses, caught fire. Three, I recall were electrical related. Her newest house was off a long dirt road, which looked onto the paved highway. In her yard you would find pigs in a pen and chickens walking around freely in an assorted flower garden. You also had to watch out not to step in "chicken chips" on your way to the front door. We parked in the same spot about fifty yards away from the porch. We had to unload the car carefully watching out for lots of "chicken chips". With a sigh of relief, we made it to the porch. Nevertheless, we had to make several trips to and from the car. Grandma made us wear old clothes on the journey. Granny said, "One thing I hate most is wrinkled church clothes." I think her days of ironing for the white folks would prevent us ever from wearing wrinkled clothes. The ride from Florence to New Zion seemed long only because Aunt Etta would pull up in the yard well over an hour late.

As you entered Aunt Christine's house you would go to the front door after climbing four steep steps. In the front room were many assorted sofas, ceramics figures artificial flowers and a standard piano. To the right of the living room was Aunt Christine's bedroom. This was where we kept our luggage. This room was filled with furniture and clothes. You felt guilty adding luggage to an already busy room. Next to Aunt Christine's room was where her daughter Carrie Dell and her husband Wilbur, better known as "Jeep" stayed. Through the living room was the dining room that contained a table, couch, and television. Adjacent to the dining room was a long and narrow bathroom. You could see and smell the pigpen through the window. Beyond the bathroom was the kitchen. And off to the right was a small bedroom for Legatha: Aunt Christine's other daughter, also Mariah's favorite niece.

At about 10:45 a.m., we would be entering Howard Chapel AME Church. Everyone knew my grandmother; and they even knew our story of how our mother died at the age of twenty-two, and how she left me as an "arm baby". I was ten-months old when she died, and my sister, Christa was three. My brother Aaron was six. It was one death that created widespread attention and sadness for the entire family. Mariah said "The living don not know what the dead is doing but, the dead knows what the living is doing."

Mariah sang with the senior choir. Their ages varied from the mid-forties throughout their sixties. This choir was under the leadership of Mrs. Bertha Fleming, who had the structure of a director and knew how to get a choir going. Aunt Christine and her daughters sang on the Gospel Choir, Gospel meant "under God'spell." The two choirs were directly across from each other with a view of the altar in the middle. The church service was always uplifting with a variety of sounds such as *acappella* singing and songs that required the use of the piano. That's where Grandma came in. She played the piano for the senior choir as they marched down the aisle to pay their tithes and offering. We call this the "marching song". You know the song they use to march around the collection table at the front of the altar, to pay their tithes and offerings. This tradition was popular in the African American churches. Well, their favorite marching song was "Jesus will step right in." The words are:

"Jesus will step right in
Just when I need Him most
Jesus will step right in
Just when I need Him most

He's a mother when your mother is gone
He's a father when you're all alone
Step, step, step, right in just when I need Him most."

This song went on for what seemed like fifteen minutes. I liked it because the choir members had to step together at the same time on the same foot on the words "step, step, step right in just when I need Him most." The harmony was great due to the voices in the small church coupled with a flat ceiling. The Decalogue, a part of the AME order of service was so long. It included the Ten Commandments. After each commandment the congregation sings a response. They actually sang all Ten Commandments each and every first Sunday. I would hate that part of the service; remember, I was just around the age of eleven, when everything was a bit too much. The preacher would deliver a pretty good sermon even though the church service ended around 2:00 p.m. Soon after the service, we would go back to Aunt Christine's house for dinner and to relax before going back to Florence. The meal was basically the same each Sunday: rice and gravy, macaroni and cheese, neck bones, or turkey necks, green beans, and dessert. We would take off our "Sunday go to meeting clothes," and put back on our car riding ones. After dinner, we would leave around 5:00p.m, going back to Florence. I remember carrying Grandma's wig on a Styrofoam head, the suitcases and our identical knitted shawls to the old Ford car. Aunt Etta kept food in her car trunk, so we always had to make room for the luggage. Grandma said, "Many churches did not have kitchens to feed the congregations so they carried their food, in the trunk of their cars. This would allow them to go from trunk to trunk to get their Sunday meal." Grandma also said, "In my time they would go from horse buggy to horse buggy."

One Sunday afternoon on our way back to Florence, Aunt Etta was stopped by the policemen and given a ticket for driving too slow! You'd think she'd pop the trunk and offer the policeman a meal in exchange for the ticket. Oh well, just a thought. My sister Christa and I laughed all the way back home in the backseat. I think grandmother laughed silently to herself. You could tell because her shoulders kept jerking up and down.

Words of Comfort

If God had our family in group therapy, I believe that He would say to the <u>Motherless</u>, the words from the NRSV of Luke 1:79, "to give light to those who sit in darkness and in the shadow of death."

To the <u>Poor</u>, He would read from, the NRSV of Leviticus 25:25 "If any one of your kin falls into difficulty and sells a piece of property, then the next of kin shall come and redeem what the relative has sold."

To the <u>Fatherless</u>, He would recall the NRSV reading of Psalm 89:48 "Who can live and never see death? Who can escape the power of Shoel?" Then He would turn to the NRSV reading of Proverbs 17:6 "Grandchildren are the crown of the aged, and the glory of children is their parents."

To the <u>Barren</u>, He would rely on the comforting words from the NRSV of Luke 23:29. "For the days are surely coming when they will say "Blessed are the barren, and the wombs that never bore, and breast that never nursed." He would continue to read Psalm 113:9. "He gives the barren woman a home, making her the joyous mother of children. Praise the Lord!"

To the ones in <u>Prison</u>, He would recommend a plea. Acts 16:30-31. "Then he brought them outside and said "Sir, what must I do to be saved?" They answered. "Believe on the Lord Jesus, and you will be saved, you and your household."

To the <u>Family</u>, He would lift up Ephesians 3:14-19. "For this reason I bow my knees before the Father, from whom every family in heaven and on earth takes its name. I pray that, according to the riches of his glory, He may grant that you may be strengthened in your inner being with power through His Spirit, and that faith, as you are being rooted and grounded in life. I pray that you may have the power to comprehend, with all the saints, what is the breadth and length and height and depth, and to know the love of Christ that surpasses knowledge, so that you may be filled with all the fullness of God."

Mariah the Musician

Mariah bought an old upright Lester piano from Greer Music Company in Florence, South Carolina, in the 1980s. It was so big. It took six muscular men to bring it into her 310D Oakland Heights apartment. The varnished walnut finish on the piano made the room look elegant. The sound that came from the old piano was rich and pleasant to the ear, according to nearby neighbors. Grandmother liked the piano very much. She would position her body on the cushioned stool and play her favorite hymns and spiritual songs, but before long, she would start playing the "boogie woogie." She learned this boogie woogie tune as a child, perhaps from her brother James Brown. She would say, "Shelly" (that's what she called me), you better learn how to play this song because I'm not going to live forever." My response would always be, "Yeah, yeah, yeah, I'll get it." You know the response that makes you think, right, me take time out of my busy schedule to learn a "boogie woogie?" Right! I went to Claflin College in Orangeburg, South Carolina and majored in Music Education, graduated and still I didn't learn to play the boogie woogie tune? I continued my studies in graduate school at the Interdenominational Theological Center, located in Atlanta, Georgia, and earned a Master of Arts in Church Music. Still, I didn't learn the famous boogie woogie tune. It took my Grandma's death on February 14, 1999 for me to sit down at the old piano where I still detected the smell of her old musk cologne. I touched the leather stool with my fingers as slow as a snail; I even felt the prints her body left indented into the leather stool. Then, I sat on the old stool and I remembered the first $3 she gave me for piano lessons with Ms. Vivian Cato. I began touching the ivory keys and suddenly, the melody of the old boogie woogie tune came to me without any effort. In tears, it took me fifteen minutes to score the music on staff paper. I later scored it professionally and entitled it, "The Montgomery Blues." I credit Mariah Montgomery as the composer and myself, Eliza Marcus the arranger. How strange, what took a lifetime of excuses only required fifteen minutes of my time. Now, I truly understand the phrase, "Don't put off tomorrow what you can do today."

The Montgomery Blues
composer: Mariah Montgomery
arr. by Eliza Marcus

Grandma's Famous Sayings

(Here are a few sayings Grandma said more than once)

- Save some money; never spend to your last dime
- Change the curtains in your house at least twice a year, during spring/winter; always starch and iron them before putting them back up."
- I promised my daughter Willie Lou, on her death-bed, that 1 would take care of her children.
- Dust your furniture.
- Always wear clean underwear! You never know when you have to go to the hospital."
- When you play the piano, Shelly! Make the people shout."
- Always get yourself an Easter outfit
- Don't bring me no real flowers, bring artificial ones.
- Always keep a clean kitchen, living room, and bathroom because you'll never know who you'll bring home
- Go to church.
- If you cook a tough hen, put a nail in the pot and it will be tender.
- Take care of your children.
- Obey the Ten Commandments.
- Everybody ought to get a taste of marriage.
- The early bird gets the worm.
- Always do your best.
- Change out of your school clothes and into your play ones.
- Change out of your shoes, too
- See here now! Don't make me get my stick.
- Iron your clothes; don't go out wrinkled-up.
- If you can smell yourself, others can too.
- Go to bed with a clear conscience.
- That gal is in a family way (pregnant).
- Never go to a funeral sick, because you may be the next to die.
- If it rains at a wedding, the couple will not stay married.
- If an alcoholic dies, and you see him in your dream, you need to put some alcohol on the floor or ground so that he can drink and leave you alone.
- There's nothing good out in the streets all times of night but trouble.
- If you are Nice Nasty, you are too particular about the preparation of food, looks, etc . . .
- Try to keep your spouse.

- You've got to love somebody.
- A child mouthing off to an adult is a Manish (disrespectful) child.
- Someone hot for the opposite sex is called fresh.
- Always bring me something when you visit; it's respectful.
- Don't let your children have their own way.
- You got to be firm in raising a child.
- I can't see that child taking over my house!
- Make do.
- Always offer your company something to drink and cook them something to eat, if they are hungry.
- Learn as much as you can in school.
- Every time I look around you asking for money!
- When you cook a tough Hen, put a nail in the pot, this will make it tender.
- Always wash out the tub.
- Mop your floor weekly.
- When you finish washing the dishes, clean the stove, wash the refrigerator, wipe the cabinets, and sweep the floor.
- Don't talk so much.
- Do! Shelly.
- Mind your manners!
- Don't wear out your welcome, meant you stayed too long at someone's house
- Don't be in a hurry all the time.
- Every dog has its day, meant bad things you do will come back to you.
- Make sure you get life insurance.
- Regarding money, if you hold your hand too tightly, nothing can come in and nothing can go out.
- Good God! I'll take nothing for that, Chrissy.
- I feel like a fish out of water.
- Make sure you have a new calendar up before the New Year or you will have bad luck.
- Always prepare a New Year's meal; peas for currency and collards for bills.
- Make sure your house is cleaned up before the New Year comes in or else it will be messy all year long. Don't forget to take out the trash.
- Don't let the New Year come in with you broke, financially.
- I'm going to Maxwell Grove Baptist Church for "Watch Night Service.
- You'll miss me when I'm gone.

About the Author . . .

Eliza Marcus is a Music Educator. She received her Bachelor's degree in Music Education from Claflin College in Orangeburg, South Carolina in 1985. She earned a Master of Arts in Church Music degree from the Interdenominational Theological Center, in Atlanta, Georgia in 1998 and a Doctorate of Music Psychology from Calamus International University in 2007. Eliza has written a piano book called "The Four Seasons," and is proud to have completed her first memoir, "Dedah Queen." This is a story about her grandmother, Mariah Montgomery, who demonstrated stalwart ability in both her life and career.

Eliza currently lives in Atlanta, Georgia where she continues to write both music and historical works.